The
Perils of
Cyber-Dating

T0154041

PRAISE FOR THE PERILS OF CYBER-DATING

**"Hilariously Funny! Singles of all
ages need to read this book."**
~ Joan Rivers, Comedienne and Best Selling Author

"It's like *Sex and The City* in a Web 2.0 World."
~ E. Jean Carroll, columnist, "Ask E. Jean" – *Elle Magazine*

**"Anyone who has ever tried online dating will
relate to Julie Spira's stories and not feel alone.
The Perils of Cyber-Dating gives hope to singles
everywhere with an email address that they
can successfully meet someone online."**
~ Dr. Pat Allen, author of the best-seller *Getting to "I Do"*
www.drpatallen.com

**"This is not your grandmother's dating game anymore! I've
seen too many women put in jeopardy by unscrupulous
Internet dating contacts. That's why this book is your must-
have navigation guide to help you safely travel through
the perilous landscape of cyber-dating. Don't be afraid
of Internet dating - just be smart about it. Plus, Spira's
personal stories are a hoot and a half!"**
~ Diane Dimond, journalist and author,
www.DianeDimond.net

**"Thank goodness there are still hopeful
romantics left in this world!"**
~ Cheryl Woodcock, correspondent and producer,
Entertainment Tonight-The Insider

"Online dating memberships should come with a handbook and many doses of humor. Julie Spira provides both. A wonderful companion for singles looking for love online"

~ Julie Ferman, founder, Cupid's Coach, www.cupidscoach.com

"Julie Spira's a Very Glam Gal"

~ Patrick McMullan, celebrity photographer and author, *Glamour Girls* *www.patrickmcmullan.com*

"Julie Spira tells a compelling story, shares intimate moments, and transforms her experience into means of larger good."

~ Veronica De Laurentiis, best-selling author, *Rivoglio La Mia Vita*

"There are always telltale signs whether or not a man is *"The One."* Read this book and learn from Julie so you won't be caught in a "Bermuda Triangle" of Internet dating."

~ Donna Sozio, Yahoo! Personals dating expert and author, *Never Trust a Man in Alligator Loafers* www.donnasozio.com

The Perils of Cyber-Dating

CONFESSIONS OF a HOPEFUL ROMANTIC LOOKING FOR LOVE ONLINE

Julie Spira

New York

The Perils of Cyber-Dating

Confessions of a Hopeful Romantic Looking for Love Online

Copyright 2009 Julie Spira, Cyber-Dating Expert, LLC. All rights reserved.

No part of this publication may be reproduced or transmitted in any form or by any means, mechanical or electronic, including photocopying and recording, or by any information storage and retrieval system, without permission in writing from the author or publisher (except by a reviewer, who may quote brief passages and/or short brief video clips in a review.)

Disclaimer: The Publisher and the Author make no representations or warranties with respect to the accuracy or completeness of the contents of this work and specifically disclaim all warranties, including without limitation warranties of fitness for a particular purpose. No warranty may be created or extended by sales or promotional materials. The advice and strategies contained herein may not be suitable for every situation. This work is sold with the understanding that the Publisher is not engaged in rendering legal, accounting, or other professional services. If professional assistance is required, the services of a competent professional person should be sought. Neither the Publisher nor the Author shall be liable for damages arising herefrom. The fact that an organization or website is referred to in this work as a citation and/or a potential source of further information does not mean that the Author or the Publisher endorses the information the organization or website may provide or recommendations it may make. Further, readers should be aware that internet websites listed in this work may have changed or disappeared between when this work was written and when it is read.

ISBN 978-1-60037-569-9

Library of Congress Control Number: 2009923541

MORGAN · JAMES
THE ENTREPRENEURIAL PUBLISHER

Morgan James Publishing, LLC
1225 Franklin Ave., STE 325
Garden City, NY 11530-1693
Toll Free 800-485-4943
www.MorganJamesPublishing.com

In an effort to support local communities, raise awareness and funds, Morgan James Publishing donates one percent of all book sales for the life of each book to Habitat for Humanity. Get involved today, visit **www.HelpHabitatForHumanity.org**.

Disclaimer

This book is a memoir of my romantic journey in cyberspace. Although inspired by real stories, some names and identities of the parties have been changed to protect persons or events. Portions of these stories have been fictionalized.

Although this book highlights some personal dating experiences of the author, nothing is intended to nor does it harm, defame, or slander any person, company or service in any way. The author, the publisher, and its agents acknowledge the following registered trademarks, service marks, and copyrights listed below. Neither the author, publisher, nor its representatives have received endorsements for approval of the use of their names in anyway. The author did not solicit any person or persons for the purpose of writing this book.

BlackBerry™ is a registered trademark of Research in Motion Limited.
Google® is a registered trademark of Google, Inc.
JDate® is a registered trademark of Spark Networks, Inc.
Love@AOL® is a registered trademark of America Online, Inc.
Match.com® is a registered trademark of Match.com, LLC
Matchmaker.comsm is a registered service mark of Avalanche, LLC.
PlentyofFish.Com™ is a trademark of Plenty of Fish Media, Inc.
Yahoo!® Personals is a registered trademark of Yahoo, Inc.

stepup
women's network

10% of the author's net proceeds will benefit Step Up Women's Network.

About Step Up Women's Network

Step Up Women's Network is a national non-profit membership organization dedicated to strengthening community resources for women and girls. Through teen empowerment programs for underserved girls, women's health education and advocacy, professional mentorship and social networking opportunities, Step Up educates and activates their members to ensure that women and girls have the tools they need to create a better future. www.suwn.org

M.

You were my inspiration.

Always,

J.

Contents

Introduction

With two failed marriages and four engagement rings behind me, I have been successful at falling in love with all the wrong men. Women everywhere complain they can't find a man to make a commitment. Apparently, I am the marrying kind.

Yes, I'm averaging a carat per decade. And yes, once again I'm single now at 50 and wishing I was 40. But I am still a "Hopeful Romantic" and am seeking to find true love again online. With my own personal rules of "netiquette," I'm still attempting to maneuver and connect with potential male suitors in search of a "Happily Ever After."

It was 1994, and it was a pivotal year for me. I broke up with the "Love of My Life" for the first of two times. After three years together, he wouldn't commit to marrying me. He said he wanted to marry me "someday."

Also in 1994, I was the first on the block to embrace the World Wide Web, even as my friends and colleagues kept asking, the World Wide What? My personal life and professional career suddenly were filled with dot-com excitement. I joined the first new media group, where a few of us Internet leaders met at our local watering hole near the beach in Venice, California. We were ahead of our time. We were the new technology experts trying to change the way the world operated with three little w's. I was hired as Vice President of an up-and-coming Internet company with stock options and was ready to go.

My introduction to cyber-dating happened shortly thereafter. I signed up for an AOL Account and was the first of my friends to try online dating. I was considered a pioneer in the days of online dating and soon became known as the cyber-dating expert. I created my online identities of *Pianobaby* in honor of my baby grand keyboard and *HarleyQT*, with the hopes of finding another high-end biker to ride into the sunset with. I eventually retired the *HarleyQT* account when I decided I didn't want to end up as an organ donor. As quickly as my profiles went up, there were downpours of responses and it started raining men. These were the days of the dial-up connection, and I would listen to the screeching sound of my phone line as it was connecting ever so slowly to potential dates. I would wait several minutes to view the latest photos of those I might get to meet. Every month, my cyber-bill got bigger and bigger as I was charged a per- minute usage fee and suffered with the low bandwidth. But it was worth the wait because there was a whole world of possible suitors writing to me.

It has been almost 15 years since I first started my online dating experience. My position as the Cyber-Dating Expert encompassed over 250 dates in my 30s, 40s, and 50s. My friends would consult me in critiquing their online profiles and I would lend an ear with full reports at the end of their cyber-dates. My tenure of online dating resulted in an on-again, off-again love relationship with the process; both because I felt embarrassed at first that I had to look for love online and couldn't meet someone on my own; and because of my history of falling into long term relationships where I am a confirmed serial monogamist, and I would take a break from cyberspace. I am a relationship kind of a gal and after all, isn't the goal to fall in love and retire the cyber-dating account?

Over 10 years ago, I first started writing this book and telling the stories of my romantic journey. I wanted to share my experiences and suggestions for success with love online. Some of the stories are so funny, it's hard to believe they are true. As with most of us, life became busy, and my project went on the back burner until 2008.

I had just ended my six month relationship with the "Latin Lover." It was the shortest long term relationship I ever had. We did not meet online; we met through a mutual friend and business associate. He claimed he wanted to get married, have a meaningful relationship, and wake up in the arms of one woman every morning. With his dreamy eyes fixated on me, he told me that he wanted a commitment. He told me he loved me.

One day, shortly after returning from a romantic trip to Acapulco together, it was brought to my attention that my boyfriend, "The Latin Lover," had a very active online profile on Match.com. Without my knowledge, he had been searching for women in cyberspace the entire time we were dating. It turned out he had chosen a life as a serial dater over a lifetime of love with me.

They say the best revenge is a life well lived, so I chose to re-emerge in the online dating scene, to share my stories, and to once again look for "Mr. Right" almost 15 years after I started. I now have a whole new set of rules of "netiquette" that I'm happy to share.

This book is not intended to scare or discourage anyone from online dating. It is a real-life guide to embrace and navigate the World Wide Web with fun and entertaining stories, all with the goal of achieving "Happily Ever After." It's a romantic journey and these are my stories.

CHAPTER 1

In the Beginning

Not everyone gets to experience true love. A love so strong it causes your heart to ache. A love that makes you lose your appetite due to the butterflies in your stomach. It's that rare once-in-a-lifetime love when two people actually fall in love across a crowded room before ever speaking to each other. This was my experience with the man I refer to as the "Love of My Life." Before he even had the chance to say hello to me, we were both in heaven. The chemistry drew us together like a magnet, two strangers who had to meet. We had stared at each other smiling from across a crowded room for 20 minutes. By the time he walked over to introduce himself to me, I knew I was in trouble as my body started to tingle and neither of us could stop smiling. Everything was suddenly beautiful. We exchanged phone numbers, and as I flew to Las Vegas that evening, I felt like I was on cloud nine during the whole flight. Our courtship started shortly thereafter, and our chemistry and passion lasted for seven years. I was fortunate to have had this amazing love, but with it came the heartbreak that was as equally intense as the passion we shared.

I initially ended the relationship with the "Love of My Life" as I realized I was his transition person (T.P.), which meant I knew he would never marry me. The ink was barely dry on his divorce papers and I wanted a commitment. Marriage felt like death to him, but it was something I longed and ached for. I had put in my years of love and devotion and came up empty-handed. I vowed to never again be a T.P. As a matter of fact, these days I ask every divorcee if he has already had his T.P. before accepting a first date.

Our seven-year love affair was so strong that when "The Love of My Life" eventually remarried, he was forbidden to ever talk to me again by his new wife. She put him on a short leash as they both had a history of straying in their previous marriages. He sold out for the highest bidder with the largest dowry, instead of following his heart.

After our tearful first breakup, I briefly went online for the first time to try to and meet a commitment oriented man who wanted to get married. As an early adopter of the Internet, I had professional photos taken, uploaded them, and was ready to enter the world of online dating. I was in my 30s so I was still at an age where I thought I would be desirable to a man. I chose two dating screen names: *Pianobaby*, as I have a baby grand piano and love to play; and *HarleyQT*, as a tribute to my love of Harley Davidsons.

When choosing to go online in search of love, the most critical challenge is creating your online profile. Having Mr. Right find you is like having a needle find you in a haystack. I compare it to a real estate listing. In real estate, the first week that your house is on the market is important because if it's priced correctly, professionally staged, and marketed well, it generates a lot of leads. Hopefully a qualified buyer will emerge.

The same holds true for a brand new online profile. You are highlighted as "NEW" in the first week or two, and within three days you are overwhelmed with hundreds of emails. If you haven't met your next suitor in the first 30 days, you no longer are a fresh face, and your listing goes stale. The amount of eager men suddenly declines, and you only receive a few emails a day

I was suddenly living an online double life with my two new flirty screen names and I was sure that in one month, the former "Love of My Life" would be replaced. After all, if I made it to the cheerleading squad in high school, I shouldn't have a problem finding a husband online, I thought.

The former love of my life had a Harley Davidson motorcycle, and I hoped to find another hunky biker, more specifically a RUBIE (the acronym for rich urban biker) as a permanent substitute. A RUBIE is quite often a CEO type or a Hollywood mogul, who hangs out with Jay Leno at the Love Ride, a charity run for muscular dystrophy. He's the guy who has a pretty girl on the back of his Harley, showing off his $50,000 custom paint job. A RUBIE often flies to other cities and ships his fancy Harley in a huge truck to meet him at an event where he arrives all fresh and ready to go with his leather chaps and shiny steel metal machine. That is the stereotypical RUBIE and I was determined to meet him. I was going to be a charity upscale biker chick, and with a closet full of classy leather I dressed the part and had high hopes.

Before the invention of online dating, I tried the personal ads in *Los Angeles Magazine*. Yes, I vaguely remember the old-fashioned way of drafting a hand written letter to someone at a mysterious P.O. Box, sending my photos, and hoping to get a reply in the mail one day. My brief exposure to this ended with my second date, a guy whose name I can't remember. It's funny how you suddenly have a senior moment no matter what your age is and you forget their name after a bad date. But I do remember his fancy sports car. He drove a red Porsche with a personalized license plate identifying himself as the "HUSTLER." I was a bit naïve at this point in my life and I actually allowed this stranger to pick me up at my home rather than meeting him at a restaurant. He took me to a sushi bar where he promptly started to snort some white powder in a rolled up $100 bill. Now you are probably wondering if I am kidding. And, no, I didn't make this up. I do not do drugs and suddenly my life was put in the hands of a live wire and I wasn't having fun. I was shocked and scared as the speedometer on his sports car reached 90 mph on the overpass to the Marina Freeway from the 405 freeway as he took me home. It was a miracle I made it home in one piece. That night I decided the *Los Angeles Magazine* personal ads were not for me.

It was February, 1995 and Valentine's Day was approaching. I was in my 30s and for the first time in years, I did not have a boyfriend. Valentines Day was and still is one of my favorite holidays. I dreaded being home alone while the former "Love of My Life" was out celebrating our favorite holiday with his new sweetheart, a woman he claimed he didn't have to make a commitment to marry. Did he still love me, I wondered? Of course he did and I believe he always will. He called that night to wish me a happy Valentine's Day, after the romantic dinner with his current love interest was over. I let the call go to voicemail.

I have learned a lot throughout the course of my nearly 15 years of on-again, off-again cyber-dating experiences. While some of these memories have faded, before sending the others up to Internet Heaven—which is my version of the trash icon on my computer where I send my bad cyber-dates to with a one way ticket, I've decided to share them with you.

To sum it up, my own personal online adventures resulted in one marriage and divorce, another fiancé, a few new friends, a lot of laughs, and a few heartbreaks. I developed my own personal rules of "netiquette" all from the perils of cyber-dating. I hope you enjoy, laugh, and learn to see the red flag warnings from my stories.

While I used to be honest about my age, I sometimes found myself cutting off a few years to fit into a search. It seems that is the unspoken rule for most women online and men now expect it to be the norm. As I do believe in authenticity, on a first date I usually told the truth and admitted that I was a bit older than I advertised. I added that if he had a problem with that, I fully understood.

It's funny how the perception of your age can eliminate you from finding "the one." You need to fit into a search or you are in Internet Heaven alone and lonely. I can thank my mother with her good genes for allowing me to forget that I am 10 years older than I really look.

With each decade came a new uniform for the first cyber-date. In my 30s, I arrived in leather pants and a sweater during the daytime and a little black dress in the evenings. No designer labels were required.

In my 40s, the daytime uniform changed to blue jeans with a "Banana Republic" teddy and a matching cashmere wrap. In the evenings I wore my signature dress: the Roberto Cavalli Red Dress, a dress so beautiful that Paris Hilton modeled it in the December issue of *Brentwood Magazine*.

Now, after hitting the half century mark, I have gone on a shopping spree to find red dresses in a size zero to add to my wardrobe for my potential first cyber-dates. They say a man always remembers "The Lady in Red" and I wanted to be the one that stood out from the crowd. Red is my color and I'm determined to expand my wardrobe accordingly.

Now at 50-something, wishing I was 40-something, my current uniform consists of a little black and white size zero Diane Von Furstenburg sundress during the day. In the evening, I wear a signature pink Missoni Dress. I have graduated to labels that no men would ever care about. Everyone knows that women dress for women, but that men are just visual. Men care about how you look and how you move, not about the label you are wearing or the price of the outfit. If we fully understood this concept, our species would save a fortune on designer clothing, shoes, and purses.

Being the daughter of a department store owner, I learned at a young age the art of putting price tags on clothing for sale in the women's department. I also put alteration tags on those pieces of apparel that got sent upstairs to the in house Italian tailor. This ritual followed me to adulthood, where I am proud of the fact that I actually have a manila hanging tag on each hanger with the outfits I wear on my cyber-dates. Ever so diligently, I list the date each outfit was worn, along with the name of each potential male suitor, and where we went on our cyber-dates. This exercise insures that I won't wear the same outfit twice with the same man. Have you ever heard of anyone who was that organized in their wardrobe closet?

CHAPTER 2

Its Only Love

The New York Transplant

One of my first cyber-dates was with a former New Yorker living the good life in sunny southern California. I make it a rule never to ignore emails from East Coast transplants. I remember fondly my humble roots and love to share stories of living in New York, frolicking around and looking for a taxi at 3:00 a.m.

The "New York Transplant" and I met at an outdoor café in Venice, California. He wasn't my type, but I was just getting started and thought we could compare New York deli sandwich and Broadway show stories. After some small talk, he told me his wife had died in her 20s. How sad and tragic, I thought. I felt so badly for this poor widower who raised his son on his own as a single grieving dad. I had to stay and listen to his story and be sympathetic as he was just starting to date again. I couldn't imagine experiencing such a loss and tragedy.

My "New York Transplant" proceeded to tell me how he impulsively met his wife while he was stopped at a red light, and asked for her phone number. She rolled down her window and called him at the number he provided, and they were married the next week. Was this a true romantic I was sitting across from or was he just an incredibly impulsive guy? How could I not like this man who followed his heart from the stop light to Vegas in less than a week? I let him continue his heartfelt story.

But all of a sudden, out of nowhere, like in a bad movie scene, the other side of this gentle man emerged, and he told me that I looked like his dead wife. I really didn't know how to respond and I pride myself as being an excellent communicator. I even have a degree in communications. I was speechless. He then opened up his wallet and showed me a photo of the recently deceased woman. Sure enough, she had long brown hair like I did and there was a similarity; however, she was a much thinner version of me. He told me his wife tragically died from anorexia, just like the singer-songwriter Karen Carpenter. Now I realize I may be on the thin side, and my family has thin genes, but I have never been anorexic and I enjoy a good meal. But suddenly, I lost my appetite that day sitting at the Rose Café in Venice.

My date abruptly stood up at the restaurant, and announced in a very loud voice, "You look like my dead wife" to all the patrons and showed the other diners the photo of the deceased woman. He repeated this line at least six times before I quietly told him I was sorry for his loss and gracefully exited the restaurant.

Although she looked like she could have been my sister from the photograph, I couldn't seem to calm my date down. I never found out if he found another thin brunette to fall in love with, but I often wonder when I stop at a red light, if the "New York Transplant" will be in the car next to me.

The Investment Banker

One day when I was home from work with the flu, I went online to cheer myself up. That day I met the man I thought I would marry. He was an investment banker with a law degree, who lived in New York. He was strong, smart, well educated, and was in heavy pursuit of courting me.

My mother always told me she had a dream that someday I would marry a doctor, a lawyer, or a banker (but never an Indian chief). My New York friend had two out of the three in tow, so I was in luck. And although I never received any family pressure to marry anyone of any particular faith, background, or trade, every Jewish mother secretly hopes their daughter will marry a doctor or a lawyer one day.

So when I received his email, I remembered my mother's dream and thought I would reply. The "Investment Banker" was adorable. He was brilliant. He had a cute puppy. He was successful, and he was crazy about me. I was vulnerable and very new to cyber-dating. I didn't have any role models, since I was the first on the block to try it, so I didn't have any solid rules yet.

The "Investment Banker" emailed me daily for weeks, several times a day, and we talked for hours into the night. He was my new online pen pal. He told me he was divorced and had no children. We were in cyberspace love, or so we thought. We talked about how we might get married some day. We planned our future before we even met and he even proposed over the telephone, which seemed sincere, but I was not ready to accept. Our night time conversations were a ritual and I was so excited when he told me he was coming out to California and we would finally meet.

The "Investment Banker" lived in Manhattan and also had an office in northern California. It turned out he would be in his California office the same time I would be close by on a business trip.

We made a date for dinner and were both so excited. The anxiety was rising each moment as it came closer to our dinner reservation. All of my friends knew I was meeting my potential spouse. I had counted the days until I would meet my soul mate and the day had finally arrived. He had plans to come to Los Angeles the following day and he would stay in a hotel nearby.

Then the moment of truth came. I went to meet the "Investment Banker" for dinner, and I didn't see anyone familiar in the restaurant. I was suddenly approached by a stranger I didn't recognize. I thought perhaps he sent a friend of his to tell me he was running late. As he moved closer and said, "Hi, it's me," I thought he was looking for someone else. But there we were face to face and I had no idea who he was. As a matter of fact, his pictures were at least 15 or 20 years old, a common phenomenon in the cyber-dating world. He was also about 50 pounds heavier than his pictures and five inches shorter than he claimed to be, and we had nothing in common. There was nothing to say. The conversation just stopped. I froze and turned pale with the disappointment. How could he think I wouldn't notice?

However, nothing shocked me more than when he cancelled the balance of his trip to Los Angeles and left me a message that he had to go back home for a family emergency. I understood that the chemistry wasn't there for either of us and that we wouldn't be filling out a marriage application in the near future. Perhaps he wanted to back out, but it was more than that.

The "Investment Banker" called me to tell me his parents were in a serious car accident and he couldn't come to Los Angeles as they were in the hospital. He even told me the name of the hospital and claimed he was camping out in a bedside vigil.

Naturally after over 100 hours of phone calls, I felt badly about his elderly parents in the hospital. I decided to call the hospital to see about their condition and was stunned to find out there were no patients there with their names. I thought perhaps they were discharged, so I called information to get their phone number, and I phoned my future in laws as the concerned California girlfriend to see if they were feeling better.

Much to my surprise, the "Investment Banker's" mother answered the phone and she had no idea who I was. She was in perfect health. How could this be? I was the girl of his dreams. I identified myself as her son's girlfriend from California. The reply was, "Girlfriend? My son is married, and so who are you?" I hung up the telephone and for the first time I learned what a sociopath was. A sociopath is a person who will lie to you easily with a straight face and has no remorse. It's a person who didn't care about the consequences of his actions or behavior. A person who forgot he had a wife at home, when he was working late having conversations with women all across the United States promising them marriage and a happily ever after.

Looking back, of course the warning signs were there. His mailing address was a P.O. Box and my calls to him all went to a voicemail box and were returned promptly. We spoke so frequently, I didn't notice. Never once did I call this man and have him answer the phone. How could I have not known? I was so in love with love and on a quest to replace the former "Love of My life," I got blind sighted.

The "Investment Banker" resurfaced the next week under a new online screen name saying he was a banker in Atlanta instead of New York. He surely got around. I wondered how many women in varying states he had done this to. I couldn't be the only woman who wouldn't recognize him from his childhood photos. It was my first experience with a married man, claiming to be single, playing with the heartstrings of an innocent woman 3,000 miles away. But I hear it is common. We had our children's names planned out. It was over and I was duped.

I guessed that trip to Mesopotamia was out of the question. I decided it was best to meet someone closer to home for my next cyber-date.

The Virtual Guy

I'm just a nice girl from New Jersey searching for love from my computer in Los Angeles. So, as I previously mentioned, I have a habit of being polite and replying to almost all of the men from the East Coast who respond to my online ad.

So when I received an email from a man named the "Virtual Guy," and read his profile to find out that he was originally from New York, I had to reply.

How exciting, I thought, to have this new virtual world, and now a virtual boyfriend with all of the same interests as me. I was still determined to replace the former "Love of My Life," and perhaps the "Virtual Guy" was the one. I was still cautious I was only putting one toe in at a time in my new cyberspace world.

The "Virtual Guy's" profile matched mine perfectly. We were perfect on virtual paper. Both of us lived near the beach, were passionate about travel and music, and just simply liked each other. He came over and played my piano and we sang together for hours as we sipped wine and talked about all the places we had been and where we wanted to travel to next.

Not every cyber-date has a bad ending and not everyone turns into a romantic relationship. We became both virtual and real life friends. We were in the same industry and would see each other at business functions on and off over the years. We didn't have a bad breakup. There were no tears or deception. It just didn't become romantic. I lost touch with my "Virtual Guy," and then 10 years after our first cyber-date, while I was attending a business conference, I walked down the stairs and heard someone yell, "Hey *Pianobaby*!" And there he was, my former "Virtual Guy."

He showed me photos of his new Virtual Bride and Virtual Baby all achieved through the magic of online dating and JDate. I was so happy for him. We hugged and compared notes from our lives over the past decade and eventually became friends on Facebook. See, there can be a happily ever after, even if it takes 10 years. It gave me hope that someday my life will be filled with joy and bliss as well.

The Desert Man Who Wanted Dessert

I split my time between my home at the beach and the one I lived in at the desert. I had a fun filled life in my convertible, driving with the top down on Palm Canyon Drive on the weekends, and sipping cocktails in a bikini at my condo in Palm Springs. I decided it was time to find a man to hang out with in the desert, and started corresponding with a tall, dark, handsome man who had a Harley Davidson motorcycle.

My "Desert Man" helped me remodel my condo. He found a painter, and helped with the carpet selection. I had a built-in friend and interior decorator, and I was so happy to have a new friend for my bi-monthly visits. We strolled through art galleries together, went to museums, hiked in the Indian canyons and became close platonic friends. Every week, my "Desert Man" emailed me with the schedule of local events and inquired as to whether I was coming down for the weekend to relax at my Shangri-la.

Almost every other weekend, I put the top down on my Mercedes convertible and took the 10 freeway to Palm Springs to get away from the beach gloom. My "Desert Man" and I would talk and have lunch. He was a man of many trades. He was even a licensed massage therapist, so

I started getting professional massages from him during my visits, which of course I paid for.

This went on for almost a year, our wonderful friendship, until one day, The "Desert Man" wanted a "happy ending" after my massage session was over. I didn't want to collaborate with him in that way and I decided there would be no dessert for the "Desert Man." I haven't seen him since, but one day he resurfaced many years later after purchasing a Harley Davidson 2003 Anniversary Edition "Softail Deuce." We rekindled an online friendship and the "Desert Man" still sends me regular invitations to ride off into Harley Heaven with him on his new shiny bike.

The Drummer Boy

After my experience with the married "Investment Banker" from New York, I decided to refocus my romantic endeavors on the "RUBIE" biker. I sorted through 100 emails from potential suitors from across the country who wanted me to ride on the backs of their custom Harleys.

And I replied to the "Drummer Boy." The "Drummer Boy" lived in the Pacific Northwest and had both a real job and a beautiful custom orange colored "Dyna-Wide-Glide" Harley Davidson. He loved music and so did I. Together we fantasized about me playing the piano as *Pianobaby* while he banged on the drums as the "Drummer Boy," making beautiful music together. We felt it was a match made in cyber-heaven. We were meant to meet, it was fate, there would be no other.

We talked for hours about our dreams and goals for the future. We were both divorced with no children. We compared cyber-dating stories, and then after about a month, the "Drummer Boy" came to California for a business trip and we set up a date to meet.

It is strange and often disappointing how the magic "phone" chemistry doesn't equate to "in person" chemistry sometimes. I just didn't feel the romantic connection when we finally met, but we stayed friends for a few years. A year after our failed cyber-date, he came back to California for my annual birthday party. The "Drummer Boy" was happy to fly down for the festivities. We stayed in touch for years, and then I lost track of him when he got married and then later divorced again. I hope he found his girl. He was a sincere guy looking for love in cyberspace.

The Men of Harley Davidson

My search for a "RUBIE" biker was short-lived. I had a second date with a nice guy named "Custom Hog" and a third with the "Road King," which was my favorite model at the time. The "Road King" was a rubber mounted bike which meant I could comfortably ride on the back for hours as it was so relaxing. I met another man named "Dyna Wide Glide Guy" and dated a man with an "FXR" all models in

Harley Davidson's collection. I declined meeting the "Fat Boy" and "Stingray."

I had my own motorcycle license plate with the initials HDQT to go along with my screen name and I even signed up for the motorcycle safety class determined to get my own license and actually purchase a chick bike I had my eye on, the "883 Sportster." The instructor, who was a retired General, actually picked on me, called me a princess, and kicked me out of the class before allowing me to hop on a bike for the road test. He thought I was too fragile to be on a bike and he did me a favor. Although my feelings were hurt, soon after, I realized that my Harley days were just a chapter in my life. It was time to find someone to live a real life with and toss that fantasy away. My closets full of leathers began collecting dust and were shortly replaced with designer labels including Escada and St. John Suits for the business and board meetings I attended, Pucci and Valentino dresses for the sophisticated cocktail parties and charity events, Chanel and Prada purses to go with absolutely everything, and Ferragamo and Donald J. Pliner shoes designed for my unusually narrow feet. I got off easy as Manolo Blahnik shoes did not fit on my feet or in my budget. It was time to move on and become responsible and dress accordingly.

The Malibu Man

After the episode with the "New York Transplant" and his dead wife, the married man who practically proposed, and all the Harley guys, I revised my online profile with some fresh new photos to go with my new wardrobe.

Since I was now over 40, I followed the online unwritten rule of claiming I was younger and I somehow stayed in my 30s for a few more months to fit into an acceptable search.

In order to keep all of the responses organized, I created a spreadsheet in Microsoft Excel with names of the numerous men I would never meet. A notebook would no longer be sufficient. It was good for my ego to have an overwhelming response to my online ad, but I didn't have the time to focus on my cyber-dates. I was in heavy career mode as Executive Vice President of a dot-com in the process of going public. I needed an easy format to decide who I wanted to respond to.

I met my male suitors in the lobby of Shutters Hotel in Santa Monica after work. It was just a short block away from my office and had a beautiful ocean view. One by one they got interviewed and never made the cut. Either they didn't look anything like their photos, hadn't had a transition relationship yet, were still in love with someone else, or I just wasn't attracted to them. Off to Internet heaven I sent them.

Then, I met the "Malibu Man." The "Malibu Man" did not actually live in Malibu, but I liked his screen name and thought he lived up the coast. He was a nice looking guy, at least from the photos he sent me. He told me his wife had died in a tragic accident a year earlier and he was raising his young daughter on his own. It was a heartbreaking story, as he told me the details of how she had been sitting on a rocky cliff watching the water, and a large wave engulfed her and she was thrown out to sea. I don't know how these men find me, but I am always willing to lend a sympathetic ear. I told him about my previous experience with a widower, and wanted to make sure I did not look like his dead wife. When I found out that she was a blonde, and since I am a brunette, I felt it was safe to move forward. After a month of correspondence, phone calls, emails, and instant messages with the "Malibu Man" it was time to meet. My anticipation was at an all-time high.

The "Malibu Man" came to Santa Monica, and we met on Third Street Promenade, a walking street that replaced Venice Beach as the place to go and stroll in Southern California. He handed me a blue box with a white ribbon as a present. Now what girl wouldn't get excited opening a blue box from Tiffany? Inside was a beautiful sterling silver necklace with a heart to prove his feelings for the woman he was about to meet.

It turned out that the "Malibu Man" didn't look exactly like his photos. Very few do. Actually, he was a few inches shorter and about 25 pounds heavier than he claimed, a minor detail, or so he thought. With cyber-dating, it's important to note that many women don't reveal their accurate ages and weight, while frequently men don't advertise their correct weight, hair, income, or height if they are on the short side. I enjoyed our conversations when we were seated, but as soon as he stood up, he was unable to hide his beer gut, and I found myself towering over him, even though I'm only five foot three.

I tried to get over the shallow stuff and we met for lunch again the following day; this time he brought his beautiful five year old daughter with him. When this sweet motherless child asked me ever so innocently, "Are you going to be my new mommy?" I hugged her with tears, and told her, "I didn't think so." I wasn't ready to be an instant mom to the child of a stranger I had only met the day before. I felt badly for their loss, but I returned the Tiffany necklace he gave me, and never spoke to him again.

I wondered why there weren't rule books for single parents, and how confusing it was to children when a new potential "mom" arrived at a restaurant. Just how many other women received a sterling silver heart while they were being interviewed to be a replacement wife and mother? I wasn't ready to sign up and I wished him the best.

CHAPTER 3

Second Time Around

After a short run with Love@AOL, the former "Love of My Life" came back to me. Isn't it funny that when you have finally have moved on, that some type of radar that notifies your lost love to magically resurface and try to get you back? Apparently the girlfriend after me left him for the same reason I did. He just couldn't make a commitment. She only gave it one year.

I was reluctant to get back together with the man who broke my heart, but that magic and chemistry was still there. It could not be denied. He said he never stopped loving me. So I put a toe in, and then a few other toes in, and the next thing you know, I signed up for another three years and temporarily retired my online dating account. Why didn't anyone warn me that you can't go back?

The following New Year's Eve, with only ten minutes left in the year, I suddenly realized I had frequent flyer miles that were about to expire. I was in a panic and had to decide on the spot where we would be traveling to with the free airline tickets. The "Love of My Life" and I opened up the airline guide and decided we'd go to South America. With minutes left on the clock, I called the airlines and booked our trip and we toasted the New Year with a bottle of fine champagne, both of us excited about our upcoming adventure together.

The excitement in planning a three week vacation with the "Love of My Life" was all that I thought of for several months. We researched the finest restaurants and hotels and arrived in Argentina to celebrate our five year anniversary. I was expecting to receive a marriage proposal. It never came. The chemistry and memories kept us alive, but the trust was gone.

Sadly I ended the affair for the same reason I did years earlier. He was a commitment phobe and I needed to acknowledge it and move on. I was ready for the real thing.

I immediately signed up for a new online dating service called Matchmaker.com in hopes of replacing once and for all, the former "Love of My Life."

CHAPTER 4

The Architect, Or Was He Really?

I had recently seen the film *Something About Mary,* in which Cameron Diaz is being pursued by Matt Dillon. In order to get her attention and affection, he shows her his blueprints in the back of his trunk which were fabricated. He was pretending to be an architect. He was trying to impress the girl. And so the story goes with the "Architect" from Matchmaker.com.

I thought I'd take a break from online dating, as I didn't want to be an instant mom and wife to the "Malibu Man" who didn't court me in a natural way. I was still recovering from losing the "Love of My Life," and was very cautious about opening my heart.

However, I started being pursued by a handsome, charming young "Architect." I didn't reply to him right away as I thought he was geographically undesirable. He lived in the 805 area code in another county, which I decided was too far away. I was a West Side girl and already had a bad experience with someone with that prefix. I decided to permanently retire from 805 men in hopes of meeting someone closer to home.

However, through his persistence and charm, I finally agreed to meet the dashing young "Architect." Our first blind date was on a Friday night, and he was waiting for me looking very G.Q. dressed in a tweed sport jacket, cashmere sweater, silk pants, and beautifully shined Italian shoes. He brought me a long stemmed white rose, a signature of his for each first date. We dined at the most romantic restaurant in Malibu, an establishment that claimed to have hosted numerous Hollywood celebrities, politicians, and ambassadors. It was the site for those who propose marriage or celebrate an anniversary. My date was a regular patron. Apparently the local florist knew him very well, and it was a scene of many of his first dates.

I was tired after a long day of work and a drive up the coast. After a bottle of fine wine, I agreed to a second date with the "Architect." He was smitten and promptly cancelled all of his dates with other women for the remainder of the week. He was shopping for a wife, and I fit his profile.

He appeared to be a true gentleman, a man who smiled a lot and seemed to be happy with whom he was in life. He claimed he was recently divorced and had been in a long loveless marriage. He told me he was real, available, and already had his "Transition Person." He wanted me to know right away that he was marriage-minded and wanted to be in a committed relationship, all the things most women yearn for and most men run away from. I heard this all on the first date. After seven years of my precious youth wasted on another man, it was a refreshing sound to hear. I mentioned to him that I would be spending the weekend in the desert and would be leaving in the morning. I was still gun-shy, but open to the possibilities.

The "Architect" called me the same night of our first date after my long drive home down Pacific Coast Highway. He wanted to make sure that I made it home safely and confirmed our date for the following week. I thought to myself, what a nice guy. He wasn't a player who would wait several days to call. I thanked him for his phone call and we agreed to meet the following Thursday.

On Sunday, while relaxing poolside, I receive a phone call from the "Architect" asking me if I would like to have dinner with him that evening. He said he couldn't wait until Thursday. I reminded him that I was still in the desert and I told him he would have to drive 300 miles round trip to take me to dinner. He most certainly would have to drive back that same evening.

He said he didn't mind the long drive and wanted to see me again before Thursday. He didn't want to wait. He convinced me that I would be hungry by the time he arrived, and three hours later the "Architect" rang my doorbell in Palm Springs with a bottle of wine, the exact same vintage we had just sipped at the famous restaurant in Malibu only two days earlier. How romantic and thoughtful of him, I thought. He paid attention to the fine details and had style.

We had a lovely dinner, walked arm and arm down Palm Canyon Drive, and he politely drove home as promised. He was a true gentleman, so I thought. I was cautious and he seemed to be a man on a mission. He wanted to get the girl.

The next day when I went back to work, a delivery arrived from the local florist with my name on it. It was a huge three-foot tall arrangement of flowers sent from the "Architect." Now I do believe if a man really wants to impress a woman after a first date that sending flowers or bringing them with you on a future date goes a long way. Women just love romance and thoughtful gestures, but it was a little over the top.

Everyone in my office stared in shock as it appeared the whole floral shop was delivered to my desk. I was overwhelmed and slightly nervous, but at the same time, I was flattered.

Every Monday, the same florist would arrive with a new extravagant arrangement bigger than the week before.

My office started looking like a funeral parlor, and every secretary's desk had flowers on it from the "Architect." I asked him to slow down the speed, but he wouldn't hear of it. My co-workers suggested that I buy stock in FTD.

On the third date, I requested that my "Architect" boyfriend provide me copies of his blueprints and magazines that he was published in to prove he really was an "Architect." I explained that I was affected by the movie, *Something About Mary*, and I needed to know if he was for real. It all seemed too good to be true.

On the fourth date, the blueprints and photos arrived at my house, along with a copy of his divorce papers to prove he was an unmarried man. I thought my due diligence was complete.

I got caught up with the romance, courtship, and lavish gifts showered upon me on every single date. Every day seemed like Valentine's Day with the "Architect." As a matter of fact, he made it a point to tell me February 14th was his favorite day of the year.

On one of our early dates, he cooked a gourmet candlelight dinner for me of with Chilean sea bass, my favorite seafood dish, along with homemade chocolate soufflé for dessert. It was like having my very own personal Wolfgang Puck as a boyfriend. My male friends were complaining that he made them look bad with his romantic style of courtship and heavy pursuit and rolled their eyes when it was date night with the "Architect."

After three weeks of dating the "Architect," he took me to lunch and asked me for a commitment. Yes, he was a man who asked the girl for the commitment, not the typical other way around scenario that I had previously experienced. His hands were shaking with anticipation of my response. He did not want me dating others and requested that I take my online profile down so he could court me exclusively.

At the time of this request, I wasn't sure if I was ready to commit. I explained to him that it was too much too soon. I was still recovering from my breakup with the former "Love of My Life," and I needed more time. The "Architect" advised me if I didn't agree to commit, he'd be moving on. Now, I thought to myself, wasn't I worth the wait? What was the rush? Didn't he wait his whole life for me? I told him, "The best things in life were worth waiting for and patience was a virtue." I got the big ultimatum. I suddenly knew what it felt like to be a guy.

With another toe in, I agreed to commit, thinking I could always "un-commit" if it didn't work out. After all, I was a serial monogamist, not a serial dater, and I wanted to be in a relationship. I took a chance on love. Shortly after while attending a Bruce Springsteen concert, the "Architect" told me he had fallen in love with me. Now they say you can take the girl out of Jersey but you can't take the Jersey out of the girl, so it was music to my ears.

In only six weeks, I was engaged. The "Architect" had planned a romantic dinner with two bottles of Cristal champagne and two dozen roses, preceded by a mysterious limo ride and the next thing I knew I was wearing a beautiful three carat round diamond ring set in platinum on my left hand. It was a classic Tiffany setting acquired from our family jewelry connection in New York.

I sent an email to the former "Love of My Life" to tell him I had gotten engaged. He quickly replied, and told me I'd make a beautiful bride.

We planned a Hotel Bel-Air wedding and a Tahiti honeymoon. I realized dreams can come true. I was the envy of all my single girlfriends or at least the few I had left. The invitations were pouring in from my married friends and we were invited to social events and galas around town. I was no longer an outcast in the social scene as I was no longer single.

As my career was soaring, and I was bringing the Internet to countries all over the world, my job required me to travel. No matter what country I was in, upon arrival a large floral arrangement was delivered to my room to remind me of my loving "Architect" fiancé. From London to Romania, Tunisia to Egypt, Australia to Singapore and everywhere in between, the "Architect" was keeping FTD in business. It didn't matter that I was only staying one night in each country; every night he needed to be by my side in the form of a centerpiece as large as the ones you see in the lobby of the Four Seasons Hotels.

When at home, we walked around like Barbie and Ken and became an immediate "It" couple. We attended black tie affairs, charity events, and hosted lavish parties. He picked out my beautiful wardrobe and sent me love notes every day. We went on romantic weekend getaways to Santa Barbara, Laguna Beach, Palm Springs, and even celebrated the millennium new year together toasting to every time zone from an ocean front suite on the big island in Hawaii. We appeared to be happy and in love.

No one said it was too soon. No one told me to do a background check. No one knew about Google yet. Now I am not an advocate of hiring a personal investigator or detective to check out the men I am dating, but a little questioning here and there to see if the stories check out can't hurt.

I first noticed something wasn't right when he insisted I give up my career. He claimed to be Mr. Nice Guy and said he wanted to take care of me and didn't want me working so hard. How romantic, I thought. He was the night in shining armor and he cared about my happiness. It sounded so appealing at the time. We were in love. I had a fabulous fiancé and we were getting married at the Hotel Bel-Air. It appeared to be a happy ending to five years of on-again and off-again cyber-dating.

While planning my upcoming wedding to the "Architect," faded memories came to the surface of my first wedding back in the 80s which was like a fairy tale as well. Unfortunately, the marriage was not. I was only married for a few months, as my gold-digging husband ran off with another woman. There is something to be said about woman's intuition. I had been sitting at Center Court at Wimbledon over 5000 miles away when I suddenly realized my first husband was having an affair. It's amazing that when a woman first thinks her man might be unfaithful, usually he has already strayed. I came home a day early and missed the tennis finals to find out my hunch was true. When confronted, he denied it at first, but he was nowhere to be found and eventually he told the truth. He claimed his mistress wasn't that pretty, but her family had a lot of money, and she didn't require him to sign a pre-nuptial agreement. Just how desperate can a woman be to steal a newlywed's husband, provide him with a dowry and no prenuptial agreement?

I look back on my several month first marriage as just a bad affair. I said it didn't count. Everyone in my family followed suit and conveniently forgot about it. By the time my wedding photos arrived from the big event, we had long split up.

Unfortunately, California family law didn't agree with me. I tried to get my mini-marriage annulled, but my soon to be ex-husband wouldn't admit to being a homosexual or a bigamist, a requirement where I resided. It took me longer to get divorced than I was married. Today, I wouldn't recognize the former playboy if we were in the same room together.

Now you might think I am in love with love, which is true to some extent. I am a hopeful, not a hopeless, romantic and was able to bounce back. However, that being said, I am in favor of pre-nuptial agreements which I provided to both of my fiancés before we got married. I may not have picked the best husbands, but I kept the lawyers in business.

I planned my beautiful second dream wedding ceremony to the "Architect" at Swan Lake outdoors at the Hotel Bel-Air. It was a setting for some of the finest weddings in Los Angeles. My "Architect" husband personally designed the wedding cake to match my flowers. We walked down the aisle to the music of Beethoven, Mozart, and Rachmoninov, accompanied by a magical harpist and violinist. I fantasized about the over water bungalow at Hotel Bora Bora and our new exciting life ahead of us while dancing to our first song, Frank Sinatra's, *Just The Way You Look Tonight.*

When we arrived at our honeymoon suite, I barely noticed the bed as there were nine dozen roses spread throughout the room, each in a different color, with a corresponding love note to represent the nine months we had known each other. I thought it was a bit extravagant, but who wouldn't get caught up with all that romance? From a practical standpoint, I would have preferred a few extra nights in the hotel than the thousands of dollars on flowers that would shortly wilt.

Shortly after we were married came the arrival of the dot-com bust. The Internet company I was working for was sold, and I was out of a job. There was no IPO, and the stock options went under water. The "Architect" was happy

I would no longer be traveling for work. With my career abruptly ending, I took this "sabbatical" period to devote my time to charitable causes I was passionate about and focused on my new family. The "Architect" got what he wanted, a stay at home wife. I suddenly became one of the ladies-who-lunch crowd and had a regular table every Friday at Spago in Beverly Hills. It was time to reinvent myself and to adjust to the new chapter in my life.

Not So Happily Ever After

Our fairy tale wedding and courtship turned into a nightmare within a few years. There should be some truth in advertising. If you were to buy an item online and something else was delivered in its place, you would be able to easily return it. Unfortunately, the same isn't true for an online groom. I could not easily stick a label on him that said, "Return to Sender."

It turned out my "Architect" husband wasn't really a licensed architect at all. At the time of our marriage, I had built up a nice estate, retirement was around the corner, and I was in the early stages of a dot-com IPO that should have been huge. Life was good and I had worked hard for everything I had. I was too busy working to notice that I was engaged to a man who had nothing. Some of my friends were concerned, but didn't say anything or suggest that he was anything but true.

Meanwhile my new fiancé spent every dime he had on his courtship campaign trail. I was wearing a beautiful diamond ring, and he lavished me with extravagant gifts that I really didn't need while he was living beyond his means. Sure, looking back I now realize there were red flags. I was about to become wife number three, and he was 30-something. His own mother didn't care enough to attend our wedding.

I guess I believed the excuses he came up with such as how he gave everything to his ex-wife in his divorce, and how she had spent all his money and ruined his credit. There was always an excuse or sob story blaming someone else for his problems. He was a big spender and I was cutting coupons on a regular basis as I was no longer working. He claimed he was a generous guy rebuilding his life. I had no idea I was living with a complete stranger.

What I didn't count on was that I would become a victim like the women you see on television news stories who tell their sad stories of how a smart girl gets taken by the charming guy. One can assume he did his research and wanted a return on his investment when choosing his cyber-dates. I am not saying this hasn't happened to men as well as it can happen to anyone. I just wished it hadn't happened to me.

I suddenly woke up and noticed things were not adding up. He said he no longer wanted to practice architecture and wanted a career change. It turned out he did not have a degree from architecture school, nor did he have a license to practice architecture in the United States. As a result he couldn't actually call himself an "Architect" or get the required errors and omissions insurance, I knew the situation was serious.

He never wanted me to have any contact or communicate with his ex-wife claiming she would interrogate me on how we were living our life and would cause me pain and grief. Yet looking back on it, she was always nice and gracious to me in the few times we met. She only wanted what they had agreed upon. I suddenly felt sorry for her and I was the next victim.

According to an article in *Dwell* magazine, in order to call yourself an architect in the USA, you must be licensed, which he was not. How would I know? I never built a house before. Although I had a membership in AAA to make sure my car could be towed if it broke down, I had never heard of AIA, the American Institute of Architects, a professional organization that sets standards to architects and claims you must be licensed to call yourself an architect. When he showed me his blueprints during our courting period, I thought everything was fine.

I believed my new love was authentic, but had I done a background check on him, information would have been revealed which would have prevented me from moving forward and marrying him.

It wasn't funny like the film, *Something About Mary,* I had so enjoyed viewing. It was a nightmare, a story I wouldn't wish on my worst enemy if I had one. The lies and deceptions got bigger and bigger until I couldn't take it anymore.

My dream guy cost me my career and most of my life savings. I was forced to clean up his mess and fend off his creditors after he filed for bankruptcy and shortly thereafter, he disappeared. He got his fresh start with another woman he met on Yahoo! Personals who, like me, started receiving flower deliveries every Monday. It seemed he had an exit plan with me from the beginning, with one foot out the door when life caught up with him. I got taken and used. My career was over and I was 40-something and alone.

One day, as if it were an episode of the television series, *Desperate Housewives,* the neighbors watched and pointed as a moving van arrived unannounced at my home and his half of the furniture was loaded on. The "Architect" is now living somewhere with "no known address." After five years together, I was left with a pile of bills and no goodbye note. I tossed away the beautiful photo from The Hotel Bel-Air dream wedding and wanted to be alone.

A few weeks later, I filed for divorce and flew to Maui, where I spent four days passed out in a cabana at the Four Seasons Hotel, wondering what to do next. I couldn't sleep and I couldn't eat. When I returned home, my master closet went from a room to house my "wardrobe" into a "war room" to house my legal papers and files. I quickly lost 10 pounds and started to look similar to the "New York Transplant's" sadly deceased wife.

With the support of my girlfriends and our sisterhood network, two beds were delivered to my house so I didn't have to sleep on the floor, and food deliveries arrived daily so I could stay nourished. Another friend came over to "sage" my house. Together we lit a bundle of sage in a ceremony to change the energy flow of my home. Room-by-room we walked in a clockwise position, humming an ancient chant to remove the spirit of the man once known as my husband with the burning sage in our hands. The grand finale to our ceremony was held in my home office where we quietly sat by the shredder, and along with the chanting music in the background, we listened to the buzz of the machine as every photo of the "Architect" that was handy went into the shredder and was crumbled into pieces. It was a cleansing experience. It's amazing the power of your girlfriends when you are in need. I knew life wasn't over. I just had to start over again, a little older and a whole lot wiser.

The lesson I learned from this experience is that with an individual of that nature, no one gets involved and comes out unscathed. I learned how important it is to trust your instincts and take your time while being romanced. I learned the hard way what can happen when you get married on the rebound and end up with a dishonest man. I am sure I am not alone with a story like this, but the moral of the story is this: don't get engaged in six weeks to someone you really don't know. True love takes time to grow, and if it is true, it can last a lifetime. Again, I remain a hopeful but cautious romantic.

It took me years to get over this experience. It was a painful lesson for me, but life wasn't over. I felt badly for every man I had a date with during the following year. I questioned each male suitor about their livelihood and past as if they were in a deposition to find out if they really were who they said they were. I never wanted to go online again after my cyberspace nightmare. I knew so many who had happy marriages to those they met online. I was the first online divorce that I knew of.

I thought I did my due diligence with the blueprints with the "Architect," but it just wasn't enough. How could

I not notice that I was being played? I was an intelligent, well-educated, successful business woman. I still wonder how I can help others in preventing a situation like mine from arising in their lives. Perhaps this book will help someone someday in knowing they aren't alone, or will help them see and acknowledge the red flags before it is too late.

They say time heals all wounds, and within a year, with the help from a man of medicine and a real life healer, so did mine.

CHAPTER 5

The New York Times Wedding Announcement

I don't usually talk about my first marriage. As I previously stated, no one in my family ever mentions it. It is as if it never happened. We just all forgot about it. It was something of a blip that happened in the 80s.

However, as a young girl growing up in the suburbs of New York City in a little town across the George Washington Bridge in New Jersey, I had a big dream. I knew that someday I would get married and my announcement would appear in the wedding section of *The New York Times*. Other relatives of mine had been in *The New York Times* and on Page Six of *The Post* over the years. I was only interested in appearing in the wedding section. As I played with my

Barbie dolls, I knew one day there would be a Ken for me and *The New York Times* would want to know.

When I started dating the former playboy, who told me he had a crush on me for years, I didn't see marriage in our future. He was a man who liked the chase, but he had a bit of a reputation as a womanizer. He kept claiming he was a changed man who only wanted one woman, and that woman was me. He said it a little too often to try to convince himself of the fact.

Every day for six months he asked me to marry him, and I politely declined. He was serious and in full pursuit. His marriage proposal was nothing short of grand. One day when we were taking a beach walk he asked me to look up in the sky and there on a clear blue day as I stared at the skywriting, he asked me to marry for him for one last time. As everyone in Santa Monica watched the letters appear for my marriage proposal, I said "yes."

My new fiancé had sat next to a rabbi on an airplane during one of our trips to New York and the next thing I knew he decided to convert to Judaism. I did not request or require this of him. He felt strongly about the religion and our marriage and he made his conversion a number one project. He wanted to be a Jew.

As our wedding date was getting closer, thoughts of *The New York Times* announcement moved to the top of my list. I used my connections, career accomplishments, and begged and submitted my country club wedding to *The New York Times*. As a successful sales and marketing executive, it is rare that my projects were unsuccessful, and this task of appearing in the *Times* was no exception.

Shortly after my beautiful wedding, with a wedding gown so elegant that it cost as much as my first year's salary at work, there it was, my wedding announcement in *The New York Times* for the world to see. My childhood dream came true. I was in heaven. It was my first and only marriage, or so I thought.

I quickly had a copy of the announcement mounted on a plaque and hung it on my wall, along with my beautifully engraved wedding invitation. Everything seemed perfect about my wedding. My parents threw a lavish black-tie affair with a 14 piece orchestra, 200 guests, and a feast for the finest. They were so happy their little girl was getting married to a man who appeared to be devoted to her. Guests flew in from around the country and around the world for the big event.

The only thing that wasn't perfect about my wedding was the newly converted groom. By the time we got married, it was already over. He deserted me for his surfboard on our Caribbean honeymoon and shortly thereafter he found a richer girl and was married a year later by a Baptist minister. I assume he didn't mention he was Jewish when he said "I do" for his third time.

CHAPTER 6

And Then Came Google

My first marriage which was so short-lived it was easy to forget. My post marital relationships were much more significant. I moved on with life and conveniently forgot about it for years. I figured lots of people had starter marriages that weren't worth mentioning.

Then suddenly almost 15 years later after my nuptials appeared in *The New York Times* wedding section, with my former husband remarried and with children, our wedding announcement resurfaced as a "news story" online. I was in the middle of my second divorce, the one from the "Architect," when it was brought to my attention. My *New York Times* wedding announcement was suddenly the number one entry on Google under my name. Times had changed with the Internet frenzy and the nuptials I had completely forgotten about had reappeared.

How could this happen? I didn't give Google permission. There was no commercial Internet in the 80s. I was horrified to see this reminder of a marriage to a total stranger. I had just started dating again, and was beyond embarrassed. I took every effort possible to get this entry removed from the Internet. All that hard work and effort it took to get into the wedding section and now there wasn't anything I could do to get my *New York Times* announcement off the Internet. A field that I made my career success from was now haunting me on a daily basis.

I called the newspaper and begged them to remove it. I wrote letters and contacted Google, with no success. I complained that I was embarrassed and ashamed at being attached ever so briefly to this man I wouldn't recognize today. I complained about the emotional stress and anxiety it had caused me. No one cared. I even went as high as the publisher of the paper and got turned down.

Men were "Googling" me before and after my dates and I didn't want to have to explain a bad affair and very short term marriage that I had forgotten about for years.

Apparently the search engines purchased *The New York Times* archives and it was now considered a news story. How could my seven month marriage be newsworthy? It took me a few months to get on the wedding page, and now it will be a permanent entry with no hope of ever getting removed.

I was suddenly single again, embarrassed that I allowed myself to fall for a man who was dishonest, and even more embarrassed to have to answer questions like how many times have I been married to total strangers and male suitors. I made it my number one priority to get this story off the net, to no avail. I contacted a company called Reputation Defenders who claimed they can get any negative information off the Internet, and it was the one story they couldn't help me with as they claimed it was newsworthy.

Now, I am proud of my accomplishments, and while there are many entries about me on Google, that at this point in time were all accurate, I felt like a failure in the marriage department. I didn't want to have to explain two failed marriages during an online interview. I was suddenly happy that I didn't have time to submit my wedding photo with the "Architect" to *Town and Country* magazine.

I was a commitment oriented woman. After having the experience of nine attorneys who helped me with my divorce, I started answering the questions like I was in a deposition. For example, Question: "How many times have you been married?" Answer: "Only once that I can recall." With a fortune spent in legal fees, I knew how to talk the talk.

CHAPTER 7

The Joy of Cyber-Dating, Act One

Almost a year after the moving truck arrived at my house and the family I once had disappeared, I was ready to move on. My divorce was still not final with the "Architect," but I was tired of living in a war room with legal documents spread out everywhere. I agreed, with only one toe in, to put my profile on JDate. A friend of mine had met and married a wonderful man she met on JDate and she said it could happen to me. It was time to marry a Jewish man.

Since only one of my ten toes was committed to going online again, I agreed that I would date five men and sign up for only the minimum requirement of 30 days. Thirty long days already sounded like a lifetime to me. I was hopeful that at the end of this term, I would have a few more toes in and be more open to falling in love again.

As an experienced cyber-dater, once again I put together the spread sheet for the responses. I was becoming an expert at Excel. Within days, hundreds of men wrote to me. I wasn't ready for the onslaught of potential male suitors. I dreaded writing back to any of them, and was wondering how I could ask them for a background check and a credit report without scaring them away and appearing like a "stalker."

Why could I not find five acceptable men to go on a date with if hundreds wrote to me? I came up with own way of communicating with potential male suitors which resulted in my personal rules of "netiquette." Unfortunately, no one was passing the test. I really didn't want to meet someone online, but all of my friends were married and I wasn't getting fixed up, and my precious youth was being wasted watching, *Law and Order* reruns.

Finally, with only two weeks left in my membership, and after careful screening, I narrowed down the selections and met five men who responded to my JDate profile.

The first date appeared to be handsome from the photo and he had an airplane, or at least he said he did. His photo showed him standing next to his proud toy. He conveniently lost my address and phone number on the way to our date and I had gotten "stood up," so it didn't count as a first date.

My actual first date did show up and on time. He was a pleasant gentleman who was in the seasonal wholesale business and hadn't had a sale all summer. He had been married four or five times, and I decided he wasn't for me.

The second date was a visual I will not forget. He was an attorney from the East Coast. Now didn't I already go down that path? He was single, and was planning on moving back to Los Angeles. He appeared attractive from his photo and I enjoyed talking to him on the phone. My mother was enthusiastic that her daughter would meet a nice Jewish attorney from back east and encouraged me to go on this date.

Having spent years in the entertainment business, I knew a lot of the top entertainment attorneys in town. I found it strange that he never heard of any of them. We are talking about those who represent artists with Top 10 records. If it was my line of business, I would know and admire the experts in my field, so I thought.

With my divorce still pending, the poor attorney from back east was questioned in deposition style by me as to why he was not a member of the California Bar, New York Bar, or any bar, other than the one we were sipping margaritas at.

I questioned the difference between state cases versus federal cases, and he didn't seem to have a solid answer as to who he represented and what he did. His replies to my questions constantly changed, and just the results of a good deposition, I found the holes in his story.

However, he was a good sport about my line of questioning him, short of a background check. I noticed on our first date that he was at least five inches shorter and 40 pounds heavier than in his online photo. There was something familiar about him and suddenly it came to me. I realized he looked like the Pillsbury Dough Boy. I recalled all of those commercials and I was certain of it. He was pop and fresh ready to go. There was no way I could bring the Dough Boy home to my parents.

It turned out that he didn't have anywhere to live and was looking for a new girlfriend before he relocated to Los Angeles so he could have a place to shack up. He was homeless.

I was proud of my deposition style of interrogation and my new ability to see the red flags. Aren't we supposed to learn from our mistakes? Although Doughboy continued to call, I let him go into Internet Heaven.

My third date was a cute guy, but a bit lost. He really didn't know what he wanted to do for a living and at 55, he had never been married. He was a pleasant coffee date, but I knew it wouldn't go anywhere. I rarely go on coffee dates. I told him I didn't even drink coffee, but I agreed to meet him for 15 minutes before my hair appointment and ordered a hot chocolate.

In my history of cyber-dating, never once has a coffee date ever turned into a second date. The reason I don't like going on coffee dates is that I figured if I put on my uniform of the decade, carefully applied my makeup and took the time to meet someone, I would like to have more than 15 minutes of conversation (or interrogation depending on how it goes).

My fourth date failed the "Valet Parking Test." It's just one of my rules of "netiquette." Doesn't every guy know that if you take a woman's valet parking ticket and pay a few dollars for her parking, you get extra bonus points? Seriously, if you are going to spend the rest of your life with someone, you don't want it going down in history as someone who failed the "Valet Parking Test."

In addition, my fourth date invited me for dinner and didn't want to eat. I had to eat my salad alone while he watched. After dinner, I handed him my valet parking ticket and watched as he stared in amazement as if he never had seen one before. He didn't take the ticket and he said nothing. I told him it was my valet parking ticket, and he replied with, "but I parked down the street." I continued to hold the ticket in front of him hoping he would get the cue, but he walked away. It's just a gesture that goes a long way especially on a first date. And it was the most affordable valet parking in town at only $2.50. Off to Internet Heaven he went.

With four dates behind me and only one left to go before I removed myself from cyberspace, I accepted a date with the "Neurologist."

CHAPTER 8
The Neurologist

I was getting ready for my last and final date in my five date series. The day had finally arrived and I put on my evening uniform of my Roberto Cavalli red dress and headed to a restaurant on the West Side for a date with a successful "Neurologist" from the Valley. What a wonderful way to cure a broken heart, I thought.

The "Neurologist" and I had spoken a few times on the phone. I had never dated a doctor before. Our first date almost didn't happen. While we were both at the agreed upon restaurant, apparently he was in the bar while I was waiting for him in the dining room. Apparently, we had crossed signals on where to meet. I thought he was late and wondered why he hadn't called. After all, we both had cell phones and his could ring at any moment if he needed to rush to the emergency room to save a life or two.

While I was waiting for my date to arrive, two of my friends just happened to show up at the same restaurant for dinner. They had met years ago on a video dating service before the days of cyber-dating and had been happily married for years. They asked me if I was waiting for a blind date. I must have had that look on my face seated all alone in the back of the restaurant. With a built-in support system now, I was waiting for the moment to arrive.

Eventually, the "Neurologist" was escorted to my table by the hostess. He apologized for the miscommunication and delay in meeting me. He told me on the first date, how he wanted a woman to be the "centerpiece of his life." He had been happily married for most of his adult life. The "Neurologist" shared the story of how his wife had left him a few years earlier, and confirmed that he already had his Transition Person.

Apparently he had been previously engaged to a girl he had met on JDate which unfortunately didn't work out. He said he was ready to meet the "Love of His Life." I was happy that he'd already had the T.P. and I wouldn't have to take on that experience again. His divorce was long final. He shared the stories of his dating dramas from the past few years including women who proposed marriage to him and another date that didn't show up as she "allegedly" had committed suicide. I couldn't verify if any of these cyber-dating stories were true but it kept the conversation going for hours.

I told him about my life, my family, my social life, the charity work I did, and how I was striving to create a balance in my life. I did not mention my ex-husband, or even the fact that my divorce wasn't final. Those subjects never came up on a first date. I had been legally separated for about one year and it was time for a new chapter in my life. I so enjoyed having a conversation with an intelligent man. It is so important for me to be with a man I can respect and admire.

He claimed he had dated over 100 women on JDate in two years. He was a JDate machine and genius on the subject. Even as a cyber-dating expert, I couldn't even imagine meeting that many dates in such a short period of time, as it was hard for me to go on five dates in one month. I wondered if he ever showed up for the wrong date or at the wrong spot with all of that dating frenzy. It was a good vehicle for him after his divorce and he liked JDate.

I shared with him my five date limit story and told him my membership was about to expire. We ended up being the last ones to leave the restaurant, and at the end of the night, the "Neurologist" passed the "Valet Parking Test" with flying colors. He politely took my ticket from my hand and told the valet to make sure he brought my car first. What a gentleman, I thought.

Before I left, he asked me if I would like to have dinner with him on the following week and I accepted. He passed all the strict rules of "netiquette" I had set up for myself, and for the first time in a year, I agreed to move forward to a second date. I put another toe in.

The next day I was having lunch at the Polo Lounge at the Beverly Hills Hotel to celebrate a friend's birthday, a ritual us ladies who lunch never miss. I talked about my date with the "Neurologist" from the night before and my girlfriend asked what his name was, and when I replied, her eyes and mouth opened wide and she said, "Hallelujah! The psychic predicted this! He's the one!"

Earlier that year I had gone to a psychic who told me that I would meet a man with the same first initial of the "Neurologist's" name. It didn't match exactly to the good doctor and was off by a few letters. The "Neurologist" wasn't Mediterranean like the psychic predicted but he did drive the same car she described and had two homes just like she predicted. The psychic also said this man would be arriving in 2008, so I thought I still had a few years to left to go. My girlfriend insisted it was a slight clerical error with the first name, and so what if he arrived early? My friend encouraged me to go out with the "Neurologist" and became his biggest fan.

The "Neurologist" was a solid man. He was so different from my soon to be ex-husband. We started dating, and every night he called me at the same time like clockwork and we talked for hours until I fell asleep. He allowed me to take the relationship slowly and never rushed me into a commitment before I was ready. He was a smart man and eventually he won my heart. After a few months we agreed to date exclusively. I met his family, and he met mine, and we talked about our dreams and possible future together.

Things progressed at a natural course with the "Neurologist." A beautiful friendship and romance developed and slowly I brought him in to my world and he brought me into his. My friends were so happy for me after suffering through a horrible divorce with the man who called himself an "Architect."

The "Neurologist" loved to fish and took a relaxing fishing trip every year. It was a hobby and pastime that brought him joy. One day, a month after he took his JDate profile down, it reappeared, albeit briefly. Before he made that deeper commitment to me, he took a peek and transferred his favorite hobby back to JDate and went "fishing" online for a few days. When he realized I was the best fish in the sea, his profile permanently disappeared. He was hooked.

One night, while we were waiting for the valet to bring our car after a romantic dinner, I suddenly turned white and my body started to tremble. I had a sighting. Standing next to me just down the street from where I lived, there he stood at the valet parking stand, my soon to be ex-husband the "Architect," who I hadn't seen in over a year. He was waiting for his car as well. Our divorce still wasn't final, and there he was inches away from me, all lovey-dovey with his new girlfriend from Yahoo! Personals. I wondered why he couldn't dine at a restaurant in his own neighborhood, wherever that was.

One always wonders who our former loves replace us with when one is discarded. We hope the next one won't be as smart, pretty, or young. There she was, my replacement, on the arms of the man I was still legally married to. I took a closer look, and when I realized she needed a facelift, I immediately thought of a few names of cosmetic surgeons I could refer her to. I wondered, as his mother probably did, how long this one would last. However, instead of making a scene, I took the high road and just walked away, my body still shaking. I wished I could warn her to watch her bank account, but it was no longer my problem.

Later that month the "Neurologist" and I celebrated Valentine's Day. He presented me with a blue and white Tiffany box with a lovely bracelet. It was on that Valentine's Day that he told me for the first time that he had fallen in love with me. I smiled and thanked him as he raced off to the emergency room to save another life. It was a very Happy Valentines Day.

When my father was ill, the "Neurologist" took good care of him and saved his life. My father had been rushed to the emergency room several times and no physician could diagnose what was wrong. You need to know there was nothing more important to me than the health and well being of my happily married parents. Immediately, the "Neurologist" became the hero in our family. Shortly thereafter, our family hero, the "Neurologist" got down on one knee and proposed marriage to me. He promised to cherish, love, and honor me till death do us part and I accepted. There was a permanent twinkle in my eyes and my world went from grey and down to bright and full of joy. He told me he didn't need to find the winning lottery ticket as he already found his treasure with me.

I returned the love he gave to me so unconditionally. There was a happy ending to my story. My friends and family were thrilled for us. I became a proud fiancée. I was to marry the man who saved both my father's life and my own.

The "Neurologist" and I had our own little rituals. He liked buying me clothes and I would sneak him into the private ladies dressing room for a viewing and an approval. Although he was embarrassed at first, it was something only we would share together. To this day I have never entered a ladies dressing room with another man, and I doubt I ever will.

He often complained I was too thin. He preferred a woman with more curves, so we always ordered dessert while dining so I could add an extra pound or two to my frame. One day, after viewing the movie, *The Devil Wears Prada*, he got educated on the finest designer labels. Afterwards, he made me a bet I couldn't refuse. If I were to gain five pounds in a specific period of time, I could pick out a Chanel purse of my choice. It was bribery at its best and I chose the blue one.

It wasn't the first time I was bribed to gain weight. As a young girl, my grandmother complained I was too skinny and sent me off to overnight camp one summer. I was told I would get paid $1.00 per pound for every pound I gained. I recall taking seconds and thirds just to get a bonus at the end of the summer. Earlier during the year in which I sported a beautiful new Chanel navy purse, my father offered a similar opportunity. I would get $1000.00 for every pound I gained up to five pounds. The incentive here was not to add to my wardrobe but to enrich my life for a trip to Japan that I really wanted to take. I didn't realize that losing all that weight while going through a divorce had such benefits. I was delighted that I arrived in Kyoto just in time for cherry blossom season and while in Japan, I learned the art of being a Geisha.

They say that turning 50 is very traumatic for both men and women. For me, the year leading up to the big 50 was filled with worry and angst. The thought of turning a half century old made me wonder when the wheelchair would arrive. Having recently become engaged to the "Neurologist," he promised to wheel me around forever. As the day got closer, I was less concerned about a big birthday, as I had a lifetime of love ahead of me and life was good. The "Architect" was finally out of my life and I had moved on with the loving "Neurologist."

One day I decided it was time to celebrate life and have a birthday luncheon with my wonderful and supportive girlfriends. I wore a festive bright blue Pucci dress that I had recently acquired in Las Vegas. I was accompanied by 35 of my closest girlfriends, clearly the most beautiful women inside and out in the City of Angels. It was a group of women who were philanthropists and humanitarians. My friends were those who gave back and donated their time for charitable causes on a daily basis. It just so happens that my girlfriends, like myself, have a passion for fashion. With the best wardrobe of shoes and purses in town, they collectively bought me a stunning new Chanel bag for my special birthday to add to my collection.

After drinking a few peach fuzzies, I accepted the beautiful new tote and thanked everyone for coming to my "30th" birthday party. I had just shaved off 20 years without cosmetic surgery on that day. I was pleased that so many didn't realize I had hit the half century mark. I added, that "After all, Oprah Winfrey says "50" is the new "30" and who am I to argue with Oprah?" It was a day of joy and celebration to turn "30" again among my dearest girlfriends at an Italian restaurant near Beverly Hills. Meanwhile on the other side of town, I had no idea that at the same moment, the "Neurologist" was thinking of dumping me.

Then, one day, almost two years after it started online, it ended online. I was notified in writing in an email by my "Neurologist" fiancé that our engagement was over and he was moving on. I wasn't "the one." There would be no happy ending to my story. I was officially "unengaged." I was shocked and hurt that I was notified via the public Internet that I was no longer a fiancée. It was a cyberspace break up and I didn't see it coming. I wondered, didn't he know the rules of "netiquette?" Didn't I deserve better? I wondered why there wasn't a "warning label" on my prescription for the good doctor. He broke my heart and I cried for months.

All of my dreams and plans were shattered, and two good people who met online were now going solo in cyberspace. How sad, indeed.

CHAPTER 9

The Rules of "Netiquette"

In thinking about my cyber-dating experiences, I recall that often I was at a loss for words about how badly behaved some people communicated online and on the first date. What happened to putting your best foot forward? So I decided to form my own personal rules of "netiquette" on how one should, and should not behave on their cyber-dating journeys.

For instance, I am a believer that sometimes we are on a "need to know" basis and I wonder why sometimes people reveal information that is rather personal in nature.

As you know I am particularly sensitive to the issue of "Googling" a potential date before having the opportunity to see if there is a connection. Now others may disagree and figure why should they spend the time with someone if their background check doesn't add up? We are living in the information at your fingertips mode as the Internet has become part of our daily lives, and we can find out more than we probably want to know. I fully understand the thought process of checking out a date's background, but where do you draw the line between information, stalking, and conversations that should flow over time? Where is the romance and courtship in a Web 2.0 world? How does a relationship evolve if someone reads something online and misunderstands or jumps to an incorrect conclusion?

I have a basic rule, when you are upset or angry with another and draft an email to declare how you feel about the party, which isn't usually complimentary that you don't push the send button or just send it to yourself. History proves that if you sleep on it, you may feel differently in the morning. I have been guilty of pushing the send button, and you can't take it back. It's not worth a cyber-fight.

The problem with emailing and text messaging is that the recipient does not hear your voice and everyone assumes that you are waiting for their instant message and you will immediately respond. If you aren't there, they assume they are being ignored. Often, the other party doesn't know if you are kidding or are serious when you send an email. Feelings get hurt. When in doubt, pick up the phone to get that real connection.

Sometimes I leave my phone at home. Usually I don't read my emails on the weekends. It is not unusual to get an irate email from someone because you didn't reply to their previous message. Sometimes an email gets lost in cyberspace, and sometimes you deliberately send it to Internet Heaven.

I make it a point not to discuss ex-boyfriends or ex-marriages on a first date. I don't understand it when a complete stranger asks me for details about a failed marriage from almost 20 years ago while I am ordering my appetizer. I always explain to my dates that I ration my information flow, as I usually hold back from giving out too much personal information when I feel uncomfortable with the line of questioning. It is not uncommon on a first date for a man not to even know my last name.

Anything to do with body parts, extramarital affairs, and long lost loves should be saved for dessert months later, if at all. On a first date, a man once told me about some personal surgery he had on a very private part of his body, which I would thankfully never see. I sat and wondered why he thought I needed to know.

I am also a believer that there should be a "cut-off" rule for how many years you can take off of your age and pounds you can take off your body in an online profile. I have decided that 5 to 10 years and 5 to 10 pounds are the maximum cut-off limits. Now, I am not promoting knocking off 10 years or pounds, as it is always best to be authentic and tell the truth, but anything more than that is just too noticeable. You will find yourself meeting someone who won't be so happy to see you. It is sad that we feel so insecure and want to love and be loved so badly that we need to minimize or exaggerate the information flow, and our cyber-ads don't reflect who we really are.

Oh, and as I said before, I have my valet parking rule, and if a man doesn't pass the test, there usually isn't a second date. I have been attacked by this particular rule and one should do what they are comfortable with on a date, but men should know it does make a great first impression if you are interested in getting to a second date.

The food and beverage rule is pretty clear as well. It's not in good taste to invite a date for dinner and not order anything to eat, or to suggest splitting an appetizer when you first meet. It just appears cheap. Taking your meal home in a doggy bag on the first date doesn't make a good impression either. If you ask someone to meet you for coffee, you should at least order a beverage, as you will likely be standing close to a cash register. I actually had a date once who requested that I meet him for coffee, and he brought his own water. The date lasted 90 seconds and he wondered why he had never been married at 50.

We live in a fast-paced society and first impressions are everything. If we can be so successful in business relationships, why shouldn't we be able to transfer that level of integrity to our romantic lives?

CHAPTER 10

Profile Definitions

When one reluctantly realizes they aren't getting fixed up anymore, all their friends are married, and they don't want to be alone, they wonder for days, sometimes weeks or even months, if they should go searching for love online.

For me, I joined these sites kicking and screaming at first, hoping I wouldn't have to stay online for too long. Yet, I was afraid of the "instant" boyfriend or "instant" fiancé, so every so often, there comes a time where you have to sit down and write your online profile and hope there is truth in advertising in those you view.

My friends who are single think that I am so experienced at this that they ask me to read and edit their online profiles as well as pick out and upload their photos for them. My male friends question me as to why I reply to some and not to others, as they are frustrated that they send out 50 emails and rarely get a response from the women. It isn't that women are rude. We are either busy, receive too many emails, or don't want to hurt your feelings.

Still one has to question the authenticity of any male or female suitor in the cyber-dating world. Furthermore, it is important to know some tricks of the trade and the common misrepresentations in online dating.

COMMON PROFILE DEFINITIONS

WHAT THEY SAY	WHAT THEY MEAN
Male: Height 5'7	**Male:** Height 5'5" or less
Male: Wearing baseball hat	**Male:** Bald or little hair
Anyone: No photo	**Anyone:** Not attractive
Female: Age 36-39	**Female:** Age 40-50
Male: 40-something	**Male:** 50-something wanting a 30 year old female
Female: Weight 135 pounds	**Female:** Weight over 150
Male or Female: No weight listed	**Male or Female:** You don't wan't to know
Male: No income stated	**Male:** I can't afford you
Female: No income stated	**Female:** It doesn't matter
Male: Coffee dates only	**Male:** Been doing this too long, you may not be worth lunch or dinner

WHAT THEY SAY	WHAT THEY MEAN
Female: Coffee dates only	**Female:** I have other dates booked for lunch and dinner
Male: Separated	**Male:** Married and unavailable
Female: Separated	**Female:** I want to have sex and will you pay for my divorce?
Male or Female: I am best friends with my ex	**Male or Female:** I am still in love with my ex and am unavailable
Male: You are so hot	**Male:** I want to have sex with you
Male: I am crazy about you	**Male:** I want to have sex with you
Male: I love you	**Male:** I love having sex with you
Male: Never married	**Male**: Never will
Male: I don't want to get married	**Male:** I don't want to get married
Female: Marriage minded	**Female:** I want to get married now
Female or Male: I am loyal and devoted	**Female or Male:** Someone cheated on me before and got caught

CHAPTER 11

The Joy of Cyber-Dating, Act Two

They say the way to get over a broken heart is to fall in love again. I was wounded, and for months I mourned the loss of my engagement to the "Neurologist." One day a few months later, I eventually got back on the cyber-dating saddle and put my profile back up on JDate. Naturally, I checked to see if the "Neurologist" had an online profile or had moved on already. And there he was with a new profile still searching for my replacement.

With all of my knowledge and experience behind me, I went shopping for every red dress I could find to remain the "Lady in Red" to my potential male suitors. I promised myself I would try it for only one month so

I could ease my way in, but after only one week, I removed my profile because of my father's insistence. He didn't want his little girl to be subjected to so many disappointing dates and didn't feel I was ready. But in that short time, I certainly learned a lot, laughed along the way, and experienced a select few before retiring again.

While creating my personal spreadsheet, I noticed that about 30 percent of the same men had contacted me who wrote to me two years earlier when I did the five date test and met the "Neurologist." I wondered if they had gone offline and returned, or were serial daters still looking for a petite brunette? Did they have a permanent entry in cyberspace? I questioned whether they recognized me as I recognized them.

It is my belief one should go on into cyberspace with hopes of meeting someone special and happily cancel their account some day soon thereafter and spread the good news to give hope to others. However, some find themselves living like kids in a candy store. To some, it becomes a habit or an addiction. Too many people are online and don't seem to be able to connect. Everyone has a different agenda.

I had four dates in that one week I was online. Four memorable experiences. None of them knew the rules of "netiquette."

Pizza Crust to Go

My first date of the week was with a handsome man who took me to lunch at a pizza parlor. While ordering the gourmet pizza of his choice, he requested to the waiter that it be cooked very well done. He did not like a soggy crust, he explained. When his dish arrived, after eating a small piece, my date announced that he didn't like his pizza. He claimed it wasn't cooked enough for his taste. My date called the waiter over to complain and the waiter assured my date that he had given the correct instructions to the chef, but would be happy to have another pizza cooked.

When the second pizza arrived shortly thereafter, my date was pleased. He wasn't subjected to eating a soggy pizza as the crust was now to his liking. He was suddenly a happy diner. The waiter and chef were not smiling.

As a courtesy, the waiter offered to take the price of the pizza off the bill, which I thought was above and beyond what was necessary. After all, my date did end up enjoying his meal. Why should it be free? At the end of lunch, my date requested a to go box as he wanted to take the few remaining pieces of his pizza crust home in a doggy bag. He also wanted to know if he could have the remains of my salad as well. He didn't seem embarrassed at all to have asked.

He went to Internet Heaven. Women just don't find the practical side appealing until you get to know each other better.

The Colonoscopy

My second date was with a "Tennis Pro" and we had a very pleasant lunch by the sea. I listened to his tennis stories while he reflected on his memories of his favorite matches as well as his fantasy to play in the Grand Slam. My date was a country club guy, and I pictured myself at his side taking tennis lessons from him and dining in the club house afterwards. With five tennis racquets collecting dust in my garage, and a complete and barely worn tennis wardrobe, life could be good with the "Tennis Pro."

During our conversation, he mentioned that he just celebrated his birthday that week. As one who loves to celebrate birthdays, I asked him if he did anything special and if he had a nice birthday. I was not prepared for the "Tennis Pro's" response which was, "No, um, not really. It wasn't too good at all." Naturally, I asked, "Why not?" He answered with a long explanation of how he had a colonoscopy on his birthday and that the day before he spent mostly in the bathroom with his prescribed liquid diet. I had a beautiful meal sitting in front of me while he described in great detail how many trips he took to the toilet in between sipping the liquid he needed to take for the preparation. I wondered why he thought I needed to know. My racquets are still collecting dust in my garage.

Many months later, I heard on the news that a new procedure was announced and you could now have a "virtual colonoscopy." My ears perked up when I heard the story and I thought back to that sunny day overlooking the Pacific Ocean near the Santa Monica Pier with the "Tennis Pro" and was sorry I could not recommend it to the long lost but not forgotten cyber-date for the next time he had to endure this ordeal. Isn't it funny what you can do in the virtual world?

The Art Dealer

My third date in my four date series was with an "Art Dealer." Strolling through art museums and galleries are one of my favorite past times, and I thought if things worked out with this guy, it would be better than taking an art history class.

The "Art Dealer" wanted me to meet him at his gallery on the trendy Melrose Avenue. He suggested dinner at 6:00 p.m. on a Friday, and wanted to show me his gallery before going out to dinner. In the horrible Friday traffic, I drove from the beach to his gallery an hour away and knocked on his door to announce my arrival.

The "Art Dealer" forgot my name. Perhaps he got me confused with another date he had for the following evening, it didn't matter. He didn't know my name. When he called me by some other woman's name, I corrected him and told him what my actual name was. He insisted that I was wrong. Naturally after all of these years and with a valid passport always handy, I was well aware of my first name. He told me to wait a minute while he checked his Palm Pilot to see what my name really was. Finally he agreed with me that I was correct about my name and apologized after his portable device made the confirmation. He didn't make the best first impression.

I did enjoy looking at his gallery and the work he was doing for an upcoming exhibition. However, I soon realized that he wasn't interested in a date with me. He only wanted to sell me art! He hadn't had a sale in two weeks. I felt under high pressure from him, and advised him that I did not have any wall space left in my home for art. He kept rattling off edition numbers and price tags and I wanted to leave.

Since he had invited me for dinner, and I drove one hour in traffic to see him, I decided the least he could do was feed me. We walked down Melrose to a well-established restaurant, which was completely empty. He requested to sit in the bar, not in the restaurant, yet another bad sign. When the "Art Dealer" went to the men's room, the waitress came by our table in the bar area and provided me with two menus, one for me and one for my date, who decided he didn't want to eat. He hadn't made an art sale to me and he didn't think he was going to get a return on his investment. I ordered a glass of Perrier-Jouet champagne and he ordered a glass of tap water. As I looked at the menu and he questioned if I was actually going to order food, and I replied with, "You can't expect me to drink on an empty stomach when you invited me for dinner." He then suggested we split an appetizer, another broken rule. Three appetizers and two glasses of champagne later, I left the restaurant.

He said he wanted to get together again, but I never heard from him and haven't stepped foot in his gallery again.

Oy Vey!

Oy Vey is a Yiddish phrase. I heard my grandparents say it every time I brought home a new boyfriend who wasn't Jewish or when I ate meat on the dairy plates by mistake. I didn't really know what it meant so I never used the term, but when I received an email from my potential JDate, with the profile named "Oy Vey," I almost didn't reply.

I wondered if he was a religious man and kept a kosher home. I wondered if Yiddish was his first language and if he was learning to speak English. My curiosity finally got to me, so before I wrote back to the man whose screen name was "Oy Vey," I decided to look up the definition in my online dictionary.

I found out that it meant "Oh, woe is me!" Still confused as to why I received this email, out of respect for my late departed grandparents, I decided to write back to this man, in English of course.

"Oy Vey" had previously written to me two years earlier and I had taken a pass on him once I met the "Neurologist" and retired from cyber-dating. Now I do admire a man who is persistent. After speaking with him on the phone, realizing he had a sense of humor, and making sure he was not a religious fanatic, I agreed to meet "Oy Vey" for dinner at a restaurant of his choice. I still wondered if he would be wearing a yarmulke on our first date, but didn't want to insult him.

I arrived on time, and asked the hostess if my date had arrived. She replied that there was no reservation made under his name. She politely told me she could have me seated and would bring him to the table upon his arrival.

Living in a high-tech world, if you are running late for a date, it is appropriate to call the other party. Everyone has a cell phone, or an iPhone, or a BlackBerry these days. I decide to call "Oy Vey" and let him know I was there. He answered and told me he was already at the restaurant and was seated in the bar.

My date was escorted to the table. I was dressed in a beautiful brand new red Diane Von Furstenberg wrap dress, a recent addition to my wardrobe that I was debuting that evening. My hair was perfectly styled and shiny, my makeup was fresh. I looked exactly like my online photo.

"Oy Vey" introduced himself without any noticeable accent and sat across from me and after a brief smile, he looked at the menu, then he looked up at me, and said, "I think I have been doing this for too long. I see this isn't going to go anywhere, I am leaving, good-bye." He stood up and abruptly left the table.

I was in shock. My photos weren't 10 years old. They were very current. I wasn't sporting an extra 10 pounds. There were no visible wrinkles, yet he walked out on me? I don't think I have ever seen anyone so badly behaved. I would have preferred he cancel the plans, got lost, or fell in love with someone else, but to look me straight in the eye and walk out? Sure it was bad for my frail ego. We hadn't even ordered water yet. Obviously he wasn't for me.

I wondered if he was looking for a quickie. Was the new red dress a bit overwhelming? I thought it was fairly conservative. Was I too high maintenance? Did he not like the price of the entrees on the menu? Mostly likely, but was I not worth an appetizer and a Perrier? After all, he chose the restaurant. I was a lady, and he was badly behaved.

I went home and ate a microwaved chicken pot pie, and realized there is a reason this man has been single for so very long. I wondered how many women he has walked out on during his 10 years of serial cyber-dating.

Perhaps there could be a "feedback" section for online dates like the one on eBay to comment on when what you buy and what is delivered is not the same. I wanted to give him an "F minus" rating and thought of adding him to dontdatehimgirl.com. I wished I could warn the future women he may walk out on, but after this experience, my one week of online dating was over. I took my profile down the next morning.

I looked in the mirror and realized I just wasn't up for this anymore. I needed to take a break from cyber-dating............ and then I met the "Latin Lover."

CHAPTER 12

The Latin Lover

After my disappointment with the "Neurologist" and my disastrous week of cyber-dating, I didn't date for months. I tried to restart the career I gave up for the ex-husband who wanted a stay at home wife and then disappeared. And then one day I was introduced to a man I fondly call the "Latin Lover."

I thought I was done with online dating and wanted to meet a man that that someone actually knew. We were introduced via email through a mutual friend. After a few weeks of exchanging emails, I finally accepted an invitation to meet him at a business mixer on the West Side.

My purpose was purely business. I was reinventing myself and wanted a new career. He kindly offered to help me with my new consulting practice. We spoke about business for about a half-hour, and then suddenly the "Latin Lover" stood up and looked at me in my new red dress and asked me out for a date. It must have been the uniform I was wearing, I thought. It caught me completely off guard, but the chemistry was certainly noticeable.

He knew all along his intentions were social and possibly romantic. He was just waiting for the right moment, and as I was leaving, I agreed to go out on a date with him. I happily drove home feeling a bit lightheaded and felt like a little girl again.

There was a familiar feeling about the "Latin Lover." His personality, style, looks, and mannerisms reminded me of the former "Love of My Life," and I knew I could be in trouble.

At first, I forgot about the conversation I had with the psychic in 2005. I was a one-time client of hers while going through my divorce with the man who called himself an "Architect." I was seeking guidance as to when all of the bad things that were happening would end and wanted to know what she saw for me personally and professionally. The psychic told me of a Latin man I would meet in 2008. I complained to her that I didn't want to wait three years to meet this man. She apologized that there would be a delay and said it would be worth the wait.

She told me he would have two cars and that one would be a Porsche. She added that he would have two homes, and he would be of Mediterranean descent and would have relatives in Italy and Spain. She gave me his first name, and said that if the name wasn't exact, that it would start with the same initial as the name she provided. So when I met the "Neurologist", later in 2005, who drove the car she described and had the same initial she mentioned, I thought he was the guy and had come earlier than expected.

And so almost three years after I spoke to the knowledgeable psychic, a man magically appeared with the same exact first name she was so sure of, drove the same car she described, lived in two cities, and was of Mediterranean descent. He arrived exactly on schedule. How could she have been so sure? I wondered if he was really "the one" as on the following week, he called and cancelled our date. I quickly forgot about him as well as the psychic and her false promises.

Weeks later, the "Latin Lover" reappeared at a holiday luncheon I was attending where I was once again wearing my signature color of red. He was seated at another table, and although he had started his meal, he requested to be seated next to me in the seat that was coincidently still vacant.

According to my girlfriend seated on my left, he couldn't keep his eyes off of me. I was blushing to match my dress. He was a man zoning in on his prey. He apologized for canceling our previous date and asked if he could have the opportunity to make it up to me.

He seemed sincere, so I agreed to have dinner with him in the following week. We talked for hours about music, life, love, and sipped fine champagne while listening to live jazz at one of his favorite spots. We toasted to our "first date." We connected on a spiritual level.

He drove me home and like a true gentleman, he asked me for a second date before the evening was over. He wanted me to attend a black tie gala with at his social club just a few weeks away. I graciously accepted, and he said perhaps we might even get together before that. There was no good night kiss, just a thank you, and I fell asleep with a smile on my face.

A few days later, I heard from the "Latin Lover" via email wishing me a Happy New Year. The following week we went on our second date to the same restaurant where the "Architect" had proposed to me. We sipped Vueve Clicquot French champagne again and talked for hours.

He told me he was looking for a meaningful relationship, had been married once before, and wanted to get married again. He said he was committed to personal growth, and was a graduate of Dr. Pat Allen's relationship seminars and even read her book *Getting to "I Do,"* not once, but twice!

I had never heard of any man who read that book. While most men run from books like that, it was a bible to us single girls. I appreciated his openness on the subject of love, romance, and personal growth. I thought he was a psychologically developed and spiritually aware man. He wanted to better his life, be a good partner, and have a lasting marriage. The more I heard, the more I wanted to get to know this man who was ready to meet the "Love of His Life."

Two days later we had our third date, and finally on date number four he arrived with two dozen roses, dressed so handsomely in an Italian tuxedo for our big date. I made a grand entrance and came down the staircase feeling like Cinderella going to the ball wearing a black satin and velvet gown designed by Tadashi. The theme for the evening was James Bond. As we listened to the music from the 007 theme songs, it was clear that he was my Bond guy and I was his Bond girl. We looked and felt like we were in a movie and had our first photo taken together as a couple. It was fun and I felt alive again.

We danced the night away like Fred Astaire and Ginger Rogers and noticed no one. We couldn't keep our eyes off each other. He later confessed that he taught dance lessons at Arthur Murray dance studio many years earlier. I was secretly wondering if we should fill out an application to be contestants on *Dancing with the Stars*. We sipped champagne, which was becoming a regular habit, and had an eight hour date which resulted in our very first kiss. The chemistry was there and we both knew it. It took us over a month to get to the first date and another month to have our first kiss, but it was worth the wait. He went home like a true gentleman, and our love affair grew shortly afterwards.

The following week we shared an emotional and enriching musical experience together. We sat in the orchestra at the Frank Geary designed Disney Concert Hall listening to the famous violinist and conductor Itzak Perlman. It was as if we were the only ones in attendance. Afterwards, we sipped more champagne at the Hotel Bel-Air, where eight years earlier I had been married to the "Architect." We held hands non-stop and had a serious crush.

We went to the celebrity filled opening of the new contemporary art building at the Los Angeles County Museum of Art and were attached at the hip.

When Valentine's Day came, my "Latin Lover" planned a surprise romantic trip and told me only to bring a toothbrush. How sexy and exciting! Before this romantic rendezvous, we had the commitment "talk" where we both agreed to be in a monogamous and exclusive relationship. He told me I was the only one. He took me to a five-star beachside hotel on February 14th, and we sipped champagne and fed each other chocolate covered strawberries. We ordered "In Room Dining," formerly known as "Room Service." We giggled and laughed, and I wore another new bright red dress for the occasion.

Every moment together for us was special. We were so excited about our new relationship. He told me that he never felt this way about a woman before, and I believed him. I believe he believed his own words when he was in the moment. And for once, I was able to live in the moment as well. He told me that he had a business conference scheduled for the following year at the same hotel and wanted me to come back with him. He kept making plans for future dates, months, and years away. He saw me in his life.

The "Latin Lover" was a great drug for me after a failed engagement. Although we didn't see each other often, every date was like being in a romance novel. We suddenly became an item. People would stop us and tell us how happy we looked together. No matter what we did, as long as we were together we were in a state of bliss. Other couples would smile at us walking down the street. He was incredibly sexy and constantly told me how beautiful I was. Any opportunity we had to dance, we did.

While I was falling for the "Latin Lover," I failed to notice that we never spent two nights together. We had a date on either Friday night or Saturday night, never two back-to-back in a given weekend. We also got together once or twice a week during the week. I never spent the night at his place. I thought I was the only one and that we had an implied commitment. After all, we had the Pat Allen talk about being exclusive and he eagerly agreed.

Suddenly, he was making up excuses every week about a family or work obligation and started to cancel dates at the last minute. He constantly apologized, but he would disappear and then always reappear again. The "Latin Lover" became a real life Houdini.

I questioned him as to whether he was secretly married because it appeared he was living a double life. He always came back and promised to take me all over the world or at least to a local romantic getaway.

I noticed that he double-booked dates more frequently and would often cancel confirmed plans he had made with me. We'd plan weekends together and last minute somehow, the dog ate his paper. He didn't have any pets.

One day, while watching the sunset over the Pacific Ocean in Santa Monica, he invited me to go on a romantic weekend trip to Lake Tahoe. We had never taken a weekend away yet, although he had been suggesting it for months. I was looking forward to it. A few weeks later, he left me a message that he'd be in Tahoe for the weekend. He obviously forgot that he invited two different women and he went on that romantic trip without me. When I realized I wasn't the only one, our love affair started to fade. I guess I should have dumped him on the spot, but I gave him the benefit of the doubt when he said he was going alone.

Shortly after the Tahoe trip that I didn't get to go on, he planned a romantic birthday celebration for me. We had dinner and saw a rock concert at the Hollywood Bowl. Fine Cristal champagne was flowing; he brought me beautiful flowers, and surprised me by booking a fabulous suite at a lovely Beverly Hills Hotel. He told me I brought sunshine to his life every day. He didn't let me down on my special day.

I had hoped the memories of his romantic weekend in Lake Tahoe with another were short lived. I continued to give him the benefit of the doubt and tried to believe his explanations were true. Every moment we spent together felt like magic so I overlooked the red flags. I didn't realize he was a magician. But after my birthday, he once again pulled his disappearing act.

A few weeks later, I got a call from the "Latin Lover" wanting to get together for dinner and I reluctantly agreed. He hugged me and announced that we needed to start spending more time together and that he missed me. He then invited me to a romantic trip to Acapulco. I initially declined the invitation as he had a history of cancelling plans. He insisted that he was serious about taking me on this trip and promised not to cancel. He kept to his word. The next day I booked my flight and the following week we left.

We arrived in Acapulco like honeymooners in love. The magic was still there. We went skinny dipping in our own private pool among the floating hibiscus flowers at Las Brisas Hotel, and spent days talking about life and enjoying each other. It was more romantic than my previous honeymoon in the over water bungalow in Bora Bora. We were living a real life romance novel. Five days of romantic bliss together. We couldn't keep our eyes off each other and he promised me we would return every year to the same destination.

On the first night in Acapulco, the "Latin Lover" admitted to me over a romantic dinner that he had fallen madly in love with me. He later told me he wanted to wake up with me every morning. He added if he had a ring in his pocket, he would have proposed on the spot. Now wouldn't that seem like a "commitment" to you? Isn't that at least an "implied" commitment? Or was it just words of a player and a playboy living in the moment? I'll let you make up your own mind.

Shortly after we returned from our romantic trip to Acapulco, while I was still aglow, a friend called me and said she thought she saw the "Latin Lover's" profile on Match.com, a very popular Internet dating site. I thought she mistook him for someone else as the person she viewed online matching his description claimed to be 13 years younger than the man who had just told me he was madly in love with me. My friend then forwarded me the Match profile in question, and without a doubt, there he was displayed in my in box. My "Latin Lover" as clear as a sunny day did indeed have a double life. He apparently wasn't aware of the 10 year cut-off rule for advertising your age in cyberspace.

Surely there must have been an explanation, I thought. Perhaps it was an old profile; perhaps he left his computer on while fishing out of curiosity like the "Neurologist" once did and forgot to turn it off a month earlier. Again I wanted to give him the benefit of the doubt. I hadn't even finished unpacking from our romantic vacation, and he was online non-stop, offering to take other women to the same places he promised to take me. Thoughts of that

Tahoe trip without me came back, and I knew I could no longer trust this man. He was busted.

It turned out he had been online almost our entire relationship, and was seeing several women including an old girlfriend. Fishing was his number one hobby. Apparently he had been planning a trip with another woman while he was in Acapulco with me. Month's later; she contacted me to confirm that both of our relationships did indeed overlap.

How could this be after telling me he had fallen madly in love with me? I quickly realized he was in love with love, and the only person he truly loved was himself. He appeared to be a player in a playground looking for more and not only was one woman not enough for him, but neither were two. Ironically in his Match profile he described me as his perfect woman. He offered romance, mutual respect, and claimed his ultimate goal was to have a beautiful marriage. After viewing his words and thinking about all of his broken promises to me, I assumed he was not a sincere guy at all. His words meant nothing. It was time to say goodbye.

With tears in my eyes, and my heart in my knees, I drafted the words to my very first Match.com profile, with the headline stating I was "Looking for the Love of My Life." It was time to re-enter the world of cyber-dating.

When I completed my new profile, I sent the "Latin Lover" an email to say goodbye. I told him via the Internet,

"It's a small world and that I received your Match profile via email from a friend."

I explained that he should have been forthright in representing that he was seeing other women and was not interested in a long term or committed relationship. I thought he should have given me the opportunity to decide if I wanted to sign up for this program or not, rather than sneaking around and making excuses. I added, "Without trust there is nothing." I pointed out that he broke the 10 year rule of netiquette regarding his age, and I thanked him for indirectly introducing me to Match.com. I advised him that I would be putting my profile online shortly and wanted to be upfront with him about it. I ended my email message with, "I truly believe life is better off shared and I was hopeful to meet someone who wanted to receive all I had to offer."

I pushed the send button and moments later, when my profile went up, his came down. He drove me into the arms of potential cyber-dates on Match.com after I had been loyal and devoted to him for six months.

I wondered if I had overreacted by seeing the profile, but since he was not at my doorstep the same day apologizing, I realized I didn't. A few days later, one of my neighbors told me she had seen my Latin Lover embracing another woman in the lobby of a fancy hotel while I was out of town a few months earlier. I wasn't surprised. Ironically, on the evening he was sighted, I was attending a cyber-wedding of a happy young couple in love who had met on Match.com.

I thought I'd never hear from him again, and that the chapter was over, but he resurfaced a few days later and apologized and slid his way back into my life. He claimed he didn't want to lose me and thought that by taking his online profile down that everything would be fine between us. He continued to make plans and promises for future dates. I said I would think about it and let him know. He became the best non-boyfriend boyfriend I ever had and called me every day and every night for a week. One night, we met again at the Santa Monica Pier to listen to some live music and to ride the new Ferris wheel. After sipping several mango martinis, a truth serum I don't usually subscribe to, and dancing cheek to cheek in a local nightspot, the floodgates opened. I told him I that I was devoted to him since the day we met, and that he blew it. I added that all of his self-help books didn't help him at all. He was unable to make a commitment and have a meaningful relationship like he had earlier promised. I reminded him that it was because of his profile online that I went on Match.com myself to seek love from a sincere man who would find his life was better because I was in it.

I told him I had met two men already who asked for a commitment, which was true. I wasn't trying to make him jealous. It was that extra mango martini speaking. I continued to babble on and I told him he didn't break my heart as it wasn't his to break. Of course that part I didn't really mean. I was trying to stay strong while still feeling hurt. I did shed a few tears and wished we were still in Acapulco. He told me that one day he knew a woman would put him in his place, and that day had just come. He said he deserved it. He apologized over and over and even promised again to take me to Tuscany and back to Acapulco again twice a year for the rest of our lives. He added that he knew we would be living under the same roof one day. He told me he loved me again, too little too late.

The very next day I received a call from the "Latin Lover" where he begged me not to marry any of my interested Match suitors. He then later left me a phone message that said he regretted driving me away and didn't want to toss out our relationship. He didn't want it to end. For a moment, I thought it was heartfelt and sincere. After all, I am a hopeful romantic. But his words were quickly forgotten, as he disappeared again, most likely into the arms of another woman.

The lesson that I learned here as we were both graduates of Pat Allen's relationship courses, and had talked about exclusivity, monogamy, and a commitment before becoming intimate, is that any of these conversations you have while you are in the horizontal position don't matter. They just plain don't count. In other words, have the commitment conversation while you are seated in a chair, fully clothed, without a sip of alcohol and perhaps it will have more meaning.

I hope he finds what he is looking for. Although he appeared to be a classic player, I will always have a place in my heart for the "Latin Lover." He ended up being my real life "Mr. Big." I know he loved me in his own way when he was in the moment, but apparently he was in the moment with several others as well. I often wonder what would have happened if he did actually propose to me in Acapulco. Would he have run away and disappeared or would we have ridden off in into the sunset together? I guess I will never know. I suggested that he read *Men Who Can't Love* as he hadn't learned anything from reading *Getting to "I Do"* twice.

CHAPTER 13

Breaking the Rules of "Netiquette"

The Secret Admirer

Just days after the break up with the "Latin Lover" I receive an email from a "Secret Admirer." What a way to boost your ego and self esteem to find out you have a secret admirer, or is it? How do you differentiate between a secret admirer, a stalker, or someone playing a joke on you?

So when I opened my personal email, there it was, the flattering secret admirer note I never received before.

I didn't recognize the email address of the sender, but my curiosity got the best of me and I opened the affectionate note. The "Secret Admirer" told me, that he had admired me from a distance for some time, but didn't have the courage to talk directly to me. He added that he got my email address from a mutual friend, so at least he could say hello.

He signed it, "Loving," and simply added his name.

The email was from no one I knew. I didn't recognize his name or email address. I didn't have any friends I thought of that would give out my personal email address to strange men. I wondered if he was truly interested in me why it had to remain a secret and why he didn't just want to call me, especially as I was newly single again.

I politely wrote back to the "Secret Admirer" and thanked him for sending his email. I added that while I was flattered to have a secret admirer, it would be nice to know how we knew each other and if we had met before, and of course I inquired who our mutual friend might be.

The "Secret Admirer" wrote back almost immediately and I wasn't prepared for his response. In his email, he replied with, *"I can't! It would blow my cover! Let's just say I'm a little in love, a lot in lust, and for now I'll just have to dream about you!"*

This was clearly a sick joke and I was not laughing. I wondered how many women this guy wrote to and what was the purpose? I blocked him from sending me any further emails and never heard from him again. Whatever the opposite of "Internet Heaven" was, I sent him there.

The Comedy Writer

I needed to stay positive while thinking about my cyberspace encounters while remaining optimistic that I would meet a wonderful man. I was smart, I was attractive, I was always devoted, and I had a lot to offer. My in box was full and I wasn't willing to settle.

I always pride myself on being an honest person in my online profile, except for a short period of time when I didn't disclose my actual age. When directly questioned as to how old I am, I always reply with, "It isn't polite to ask a lady her age."

Just recently I received an email out of no where from a "Comedy Writer." I needed to laugh after the "Latin Lover" disappeared, and after one subsequent cyber-date ended shortly after he told me about his vasectomy in the first three minutes of a coffee date. Why did he think I needed to know?

Then another date told me about a wild affair he had with a woman, and stated that, "If you don't use it, you lose it." A month later I was reading the *Los Angeles Times*, and there it was–the article that substantiated my date's inappropriate comment with the headline stating "Use it or lost it: Yes, it's true." Apparently the *American Journal of Medicine* had just published a new scientific study on the topic. Although my date was knowledgeable on the subject and the data was now backed up with supporting evidence, I questioned why I was subjecting myself to such losers. Aren't they supposed to be putting their best feet forward? Why don't they realize that when I don't return their calls, they have been inappropriate? Why didn't they know the rules of "netiquette?"

And just what is considered appropriate behavior in cyberspace these days? I guess it depends on what you are looking for, but I believe in truth in advertising, and always come clean on the first date and tell men about my real age, and my desire to fit into a search. If you are looking to "hook up," then find someone to "hook up" with. If you are looking for marriage and romance, then don't be a commitment phobe or already married. Why is it so hard? Why is everyone so frustrated?

While pondering all of the above, I answered the mysterious and intriguing email from the "Comedy Writer." It was accompanied by a photo that made me think we really would be a cute couple, so I thought I had nothing to lose. The "Comedy Writer" told me that I wrote like someone who was comfortable with myself and knew myself well. He said that appealed to him. He added, *"Oh and that physical attractiveness thing, too, that men supposedly care about. I almost didn't respond to your profile, as you've obviously exceeded Federal Cuteness Standards and I'm this close to making a citizen's arrest."*

He wanted me to check out his profile and let him know whether we might have the chance for a lifetime of mutual worship and adoration. He hoped it was in the cards for us according to his initial contact. He added, *"If not, perhaps we could just get together to have soup now and then."* He signed his affectionate note with, *"Your potential boyfriend and soup partner."*

Now I know he gets paid to write comedy for a living, but he got my attention and I secretly wondered how he knew that I usually ordered soup with my dinner. I wrote back, and told him he could write to me directly at my personal email address. Being one who regularly rations my information flow, I never even gave him my first or last name.

The "Comedy Writer's" response was even cleverer than the introduction. He thanked me and referred to me as the "Mystery Woman." He added that in addition to all the other qualities he mentioned he was looking for was a romantic partner who was willing to reveal her first name. He asked if that could be me and if so would I like to speak on the phone.

The "Comedy Writer" was right. I needed to lighten up a little and open up a bit more. The next evening he called me and we laughed and spoke for a while and then he decided we should meet. We made plans for Friday night to go to the Hollywood Bowl and I revealed my first name only.

Now you already know how sensitive I am to the "Google" thing. So when I woke up the next day and checked my email, and there was a message from the "Comedy Writer" simply entitled *"It's All about Julie,"* I wasn't laughing.

I read the email and I panicked. It turned out through the magic of Google he did a search and only typed in my personal email address. Instantly he found out my two last names, my real age, the now famous *New York Times* wedding announcement, and seven other pages of Google articles that he copied and pasted into an email. He sent this data to me. It was as if I didn't know who I was and had to be reminded. I had already "Googled" myself. I already knew.

He found financial information, my business profiles, my resume, photos of me from society parties, and more. I suddenly felt like I was being stalked by a stranger, obsessed about learning about me and now he was the one who should be arrested. It was no longer funny and I wasn't laughing. Here was a man I had not even had the chance to have a first date with digging deep almost to the point of doing a background check and then letting me know he did so. I felt like my personal boundaries had been violated. It was a red flag.

Now I understand, the privacy issues are gone now with the public Internet, but it had gone too far for me. This was a sensitive issue. I had survived the chapter with the "Architect" ex-husband and had come out alive with my head held high. I wasn't going back there and I wasn't going to meet the "Comedy Writer."

I sent an email back to the "Comedy Writer" and politely told him that he had broken the rules of "netiquette." I advised him that I was well aware of my professional accomplishments and my social status in this town as well as all of the Google articles about me.

I added that I was extremely uncomfortable with someone I hadn't yet met, searching out all the available data on Google before our first date. I explained to him that if he really wanted to get to know me or any woman in a quality way, it would be more appropriate to let the conversations flow and learn to get to know one another in a natural way, or at least spend time getting to know me and where he could ask questions which I would have been happy to answer.

That being said, I told him to find another date for Friday night. I added that I didn't make it a habit of checking Google before going on a first date, and I sometimes don't even "Google" one at all. In the days before the Internet, dating and courting took a more proper path.

I suggested that in the future he should realize that most women will not be pleased to find out they have been checked out with a fine tooth comb before a date. I added that if he felt the urge to have to Google a date that he shouldn't push the "send" button and to realize what proper "netiquette" was in dating.

I wished him good luck with his search and ended with "I'm just an old fashioned girl."

I had learned the art of writing a goodbye letter on the Internet after I received written notice that I was no longer engaged by the "Neurologist," and after I said goodbye to the "Latin Lover" in an email and took the high road. I never heard from the "Comedy Writer" again, but I hope he learned a lesson from me.

The Lunch Special

Recently I accepted a date to meet a man at a local Chinese restaurant for lunch. He chose this particular restaurant as he was a fan of their "Lunch Special."

As I waited for my ever-so-anxious date, I peruse the menu and found three categories to choose from. There was the $4.95 page, the $5.45 page, and the $5.95 page. I was so shocked with food prices on the rise that there was any place on the West Side that served three course meals for under $6.00.

While there were plenty of selections to choose from, I was only interested in ordering #35, the tofu with vegetables. It wasn't intentional that my choice was on the $5.95 page, but I couldn't seem to find tofu on the lesser priced pages. It wasn't as if I was ordering lobster at The Palm. We were there for the "Lunch Special" and give or take a dollar or so, I didn't think he would mind.

The waitress came to take our order and I chose the vegetarian dish on the right side of the menu. My date interrupts and suggests that I order something on the lower priced page on the left hand side of the menu. I wanted tofu. Tofu was not available on the page he was fixated on. I politely point that out to him, where he replied with "I'm sure they can make a substitution." The waitress points out to my date that there are no substitutions on the "Lunch Special" menu.

Sadly, my date had to fork out an extra 50 cents to please me at our first and only date, but the damage was done. How could I go out with someone who was trying to force me to order something I didn't want to eat from the left side of the menu to save 50 cents or a dollar? I knew he wasn't the one for me. He then wanted to take the remainder of my meal home in a doggy bag for his pet. I wasn't sure if he even had a pet and I don't know many puppies that eat tofu. I took the balance of the meal home and threw it away.

He didn't realize how lucky he was that he got off easy on the "Valet Parking Test." I parked on the street. I drove away as I heard his voice yelling at me, "What, no hug, no kiss, when is our next date?"

The Flirty Guy

Today, I had a first date with a guy called the "Flirty Guy." He sent me a few flirty emails. We eventually spoke on the phone and although I knew he was 10 years younger than me, I agreed to meet him for a flirty dinner. I was excited about this date and had already cancelled my dinner with the "Comedy Writer." While I was driving to meet a new first date, I notice there's a voicemail message on my cell phone and it was from the "Latin Lover." I hadn't spoken to him in a while and it seemed his radar was out. It was as though he had a special GPS for when I was about to go on a date. I chose to ignore it.

Being a flirty girl since I was four years old, I think the "Flirty Guy" met his match with me. In my evening Missoni pink signature dress, I became the coy *Pianobaby* again with no last name. Yes I would not reveal my last name, as I was still suffering the shock of the "Comedy Writer" who found out my last names by typing in my email address.

The "Flirty Guy" had his own set of rules. He believed he had to kiss each girl at the end of the date to determine if he was going to ask her out again. I didn't feel very comfortable with this, as I don't make it a habit of practicing the art of kissing with a stranger I have just met. He also liked text messaging. I told the "Flirty Guy," I wasn't fond of text messaging, and that if he wanted to see me again, he would have to call.

They say men like receiving directions. Men complain that women are so complicated, and wonder why we can't just tell them what we want. So, I give the "Flirty Guy" instructions on how to contact me if he was interested. And what happens? Men do what they love to do best, ignore women. Yes he ignored my directions. So on the following week, I receive my first text message from the "Flirty Guy," saying one word "Sushi." I understand men are simple creatures, but how am I supposed to know if that meant he just ate sushi, he likes sushi, he is going to eat sushi, do I like sushi, or do I want to have sushi with him?. I choose to ignore the text message as I had already told him I don't like to text.

The next day, a second text message arrived, which said, "Long Hot Day." I didn't need a weather forecast so was I to assume that he was hot, the weather was hot, I was hot, or if he wanted to know if I was using my air conditioning. I will never know.

The third day after our first and only date, I get a text message simply saying, "Finally, cocktail hour." Again, was he off for drinks with another potential cyber-date or woman, or was he drinking alone? Did he want to meet for a drink? I didn't know.

On the fourth day I receive a text, only saying "Good Morning." So on day five after our first date, I called him to say hello and ask for an explanation. Although he had my phone number and could have easily called, he chose not to. I asked him why he sent one and two word text messages to me all week long, as I was confused as to what he wanted to express, and he replied with, "I know you don't like text messages." And that was the end of my communication with the "Flirty Guy."

I had a feeling he was looking to "hookup" so I didn't expect to hear from him again, but I learned on our one evening together nibbling on chicken lettuce wraps, that he was a serial JDate vacation attendee. He had gone on JDate vacations to Mexico, Puerto Rico, and on a cruise. It's nice to be educated on the options in the cyber-dating world.

The One Night Stand

I pride myself on being a respectable woman. I know I have a tendency to be flirtatious, but I have never ever had a one night stand. I am as proud of the fact that I don't have one night stands as I am of maintaining my very high credit score.

Now that I am online, I am hearing stories of cybersex, one night stands, hooking up, and things that are just not a part of my vocabulary or lifestyle, but are very common in the world of cyber-dating.

So only once, yes once in my life, I almost had a "One Night Stand." I was in my 20s and I was in Acapulco. Yes Acapulco, where 25 years later I had the romantic trip of a lifetime with the Latin Lover. I don't know what it is about Acapulco and why people fall in love there or why it is such a great romantic destination, but if you need to spice up your love life, I suggest booking a vacation there.

On my first trip to Acapulco, I met this hunky Sicilian guy named Antonio on the beach. He was much younger, and just sexy as can be. We were staying in the same hotel. That night we went to dinner with some friends and later patronized the fabulous nightclubs of Acapulco, including Jackie O's, Baby O's, and Le Dome. After a night of dancing and margaritas, somehow this young Italian stallion ended up in my room, and yes for the first time and last time in my life I had what I thought was a one night stand, or was it?

After our first night together, we couldn't be apart. We were inseparable on this entire vacation. It is interesting how people let their guards down when they are on vacation. I often wonder would I talk to the same people I meet on holiday if I was home on the West Side of Los Angeles. It's a vacation phenomenon and somehow you become more open and vulnerable when you are out of town. That must be the case, as it took the Latin Lover six months to tell me he had let his guard down and loved me, and it was also in Acapulco.

I have come to the conclusion that if we were less judgmental in our own home towns and behaved and felt like we did while we were on vacation, our lives would be more enriched. There should be a rule that when you look at everyone at home, you should pause and ask yourself, "Is this someone I would get to know while on vacation?" We easily discard potential dates and friends without getting to know them.

So while in my 20s, after five days of non-stop love and an exciting nightlife of dancing with the Italian in Acapulco, we both realized we just couldn't be apart. He was no longer a "One Night Stand."

It didn't matter that we lived in different countries; we still both lived on the same continent. He was from Toronto and I was from Los Angeles. It was in the days before we had unlimited North American toll free calls and the Internet to communicate. We wrote snail mail to each other every day like the old fashioned courtship I still yearn for. We kept Hallmark in business. We spoke every night and each of us spent about $300 on monthly long distance calls. We were hopelessly devoted and every month one of us went to visit each other. I became a frequent shopper in the trendy neighborhood of Yorkville as well as a patron in a large shopping mall called the Eaton Center, during my trips to Toronto. The U.S. dollar went further in Canada so while my honey was at work, I was keeping the retailers in business. On our first summer together, we travelled to Europe and stayed there for three months in search of hotels with a decent bathroom. It was unconditional love at its best.

The failed attempt at a "One Night Stand" stand turned into a loving relationship that lasted three years. Now I am not promoting having a one night stand and hoping it lasts three years or turns into marriage. This was an anomaly. We got lucky.

After a few years, the cute Italian finally moved to Los Angeles so we could be together every day. We talked about marriage, but unfortunately he did not have a green card, and he went back to his homeland. I think of him often and hope he is happily married.

The following year, I got married for the first time on the rebound to the guy I wouldn't even recognize today, although as you are now aware, I am reminded of this daily on Google.

The Girlfriend, or Was She?

Quite often a man or woman will "test the water" before ending a relationship that isn't working out. Sometimes one needs to see if there is someone better to move on to. I noticed this briefly with the "Neurologist" before he made a commitment to me. In today's time, what better place to swim than on an Internet dating site?

So my girlfriend Jody went out on a cyber-date with a much younger guy. He took her to dinner and when the bill arrived, he announced he wanted to split the check. Although she wasn't aware of it when she accepted the date, they were going Dutch treat. I don't believe I have ever had a man suggest we split the check on a first date, and neither did my friend Jody.

On their date, he mentioned that his birthday was coming up soon. Later that week he emailed her the Evite invitation to his birthday party. The event was to be held at a restaurant where the first 25 people who arrive will get a free drink. Jody invited me to be her date, and since she was driving I agree to accompany her to the party.

After a very long drive over several Los Angeles freeways, we arrive at a restaurant in a town I never heard of. When Jody went to the ladies room, she met a woman and they talked about the neighborhood scene. The woman told Jody, "We live right down the street."

Jody wondered who the other half of "we" was and asked the party guest, and it turned out she was the live-in love of the birthday boy or "The Girlfriend" so it appeared.

Obviously the significant other to the man of honor that evening didn't know that Jody had a cyber-date with her beau only a week before.

Now Jody is smart enough to be discreet and wasn't really interested in having a second date with the encumbered man who believed in going Dutch treat. But woman to woman, how can you not feel sorry for the girl who had no idea her beau had a separate dating life in cyberspace?

When Jody returned from the ladies room and told me the story and pointed out the girlfriend, my radar immediately noticed the shiny diamond engagement ring on the left hand of the birthday boy's live-in-love as well as her very obvious wedding band. The alleged girlfriend was actually a wife. We felt sorry for her and left the party, and as Jody said goodbye to the birthday boy, he made it a point to pinch her butt as she left. He called her a few weeks later, and she deleted the message from her voicemail.

The Mother-in-Law

One day, I came home to find a few emails in my in box from Match.com. I was shocked to see that one was sent from a 61-year old woman. Although she was attractive, my profile was clear that I was a woman, looking for a man. Out of curiosity, I opened her email to find out she was actually playing matchmaker for her never married son.

She opened her note to me saying that I might think it was odd, but her son was reluctant to search for someone special as he was jaded from the whole dating scene. She assured me that he really did want to meet that special someone. She said that I was "darling" and would be perfect for her son and she thought we would be a good match. He was not in the dating service, but if I was interested she would have him contact me directly and send me his photos.

Since I already passed the mother-in-law test, I agreed to give her my personal email address so her son could contact me directly. The very next day while I was enjoying Bossa Nova night at the Hollywood Bowl with my girlfriends, the ever so shy son sent me an email along with three photos for us all to examine. I decided to get a group approval from the girls before writing back.

The son said he thought it was "cool" that his mother was acting as a matchmaker for us. He said he was an investment banker who was 43, but claimed to look like he was in his mid 30s. He added that he was fit, athletic, easy going, a good cook, worked hard and played hard, and had a good balance in his life. He said he was tired of the dating scene and lived in the Beverly Hills area. What area, I wasn't sure as it clearly wasn't Beverly Hills.

I was concerned that he had never been married, but as I passed my mobile device around to my friends, we all stared at the pictures of my possible new date and my potential new "Mother-in-Law." My friends scrutinized his photos and one noticed that he wore the same blue shirt in all three shots. No one was good enough for me according to my friends, but they were all married. None of them ever had to look for love in cyberspace. They didn't know how I felt and how frustrating it can be and too often so painfully lonely. One girlfriend thought he had nice eyes and one said he had nice legs. I sat and wondered if we would be double dating with him and his mother on one of her Match.com dates. I was hoping she wasn't planning on being a chaperone on our first date.

I decided to sleep on it before responding, and finally the next morning I sent him an email with my phone number so we could graduate to a conversation. Before he called me back, my intuition told me there was something about this man that his mother hadn't revealed. There usually is a good reason why a man in his 40s, who still wishes he was still in his 30s, has never been married. I wanted to find out more. I remembered the trick the "Comedy Writer" did to me and I typed in my potential cyber-date's personal email address in a Google search to find out who this bachelor investment banker was.

Words can't describe the look on my face when I saw his personal ad on the first page of Google. My potential new "Mother-in-Law's" son had placed an online personal ad in a casual encounters group and swingers website that was clearly posted for the world to see. The ad simply stated: *Man Seeking Woman Tantra Partner in Los Angeles.* There he was the same single guy, whose mother wanted to find him a wife, who only a month earlier posted this ad online. He claimed to be in his 30s and was searching for X-rated women, and certainly didn't appear to be marriage-minded. He wanted women to email their desires to him so he could see if they had a blissful connection. He claimed to be an expert in "G-spot massage."

I don't know if the "Mother-in-Law" knew about her son's other life, or participated as well, but clearly any woman in the universe now can easily find this data. Naturally, I won't be meeting the son, and hopefully someday I will have a different "Mother-in-Law." Sometimes, it's just good to follow your intuition and check things out.

CHAPTER 14

The Joy of Cyber-Dating, Act Three

The Boy Next Door

I finally decided to put all 10 toes in and go for it after my relationship ended with the "Latin Lover." I joined three online dating sites at the same time. I was new to Match and Plenty of Fish, and a repeat guest on JDate. I figured what did I have to lose? I set up three Excel spreadsheets and instantly my in box was getting filled with emails, most of which I would never have the time to read. I quickly realized it can be confusing even for someone who is as proficient at Excel like I am.

I went on three lunch dates with men I met from Plenty of Fish. On this site, members get to pick a fish that describes themselves. I met The Seahorse, The Octopus, and The Swordfish. I of course, was The Angel Fish. None of these fishermen advanced to a second date and when they continued to go "fishing," I ended up swimming alone.

I am not experienced at being a serial dater and only wanted to commit to one month of online dating. I was curious and hopeful. It was great for my ego to wake up and suddenly have thousands of potential suitors view my online profile and hundreds of interested men write to me.

The very first day I went on JDate, I received an email from a West Side man who was also originally from New Jersey. Within hours we found out that we grew up only one mile away from each other. We quickly found out that our parents knew each other as well. We had gone to the same day camp as kids and our families belonged to the same country club while we were growing up. Coincidently, we were even born in the same hospital during the same year. In addition, we knew at least 30 people in common. It felt like fate had brought us together. They say that timing is everything and everything happens for a reason. We were meant to meet.

My mother was thrilled, and suddenly I was talking for hours every day to the "Boy Next Door" who surprisingly enough, I never met as a child. We instantly connected and wondered why we had never met before as our lives were so in synch. We talked about how as children, we both went to the same famous hot dog stand in a nearby town. We both had the same favorite deli close by, where we reminisced about the days of digging deep into a huge barrel to pick out a fresh pickle for free. Finally the day came for us to meet and I met him at his beach club for lunch. I liked that he was family oriented and that his children were a priority. As we had already spent 10 hours on the phone talking about our childhood, he wanted to hear everything about me for the past 30 years since I left New Jersey.

I liked that he was smart. I liked that he was seriously interested in me. He called me immediately after our first date as my car was leaving the parking lot to ask me for another date. I was cautious; and had to remind myself that I had gotten engaged to the "Architect" I had met on Matchmaker.com in six short weeks. But since our families knew each other, I was hopeful this could turn into something special. I think we both were.

Although I was happy to meet the "Boy Next Door," I didn't want a relationship that would start too fast and burn out equally as fast. I really like to take things slowly. I explained it to him and apologized in advance that I rationed my information flow. I told the "Boy Next Door" that I liked to develop the friendship part of a relationship first. He was an open book. He was direct and real. We knew so many people in common, it just felt very comfortable. There were no secrets. Every morning I would get a wake up email message from him wishing me good morning and telling me about his upcoming day. It was as if we'd known each other our whole lives.

Suddenly I had a new support system from the "Boy Next Door." We liked the same music, had similar interests, similar backgrounds, and I would have never met him if the "Latin Lover" didn't get caught with his online Match profile. The "Boy Next Door" cared about everything happening in my life and we were becoming fast friends. It didn't bother me that he found my *New York Times* wedding announcement on Google. In fact, he showed me his *New York Times* wedding announcement as well.

We went together to a charity dinner one night and walked in holding hands with smiles on our faces. I hadn't held hands with another man in a long time and it felt good. I rarely graduated to a second date with my cyber-dates. I actually could be headed into the world of "Happily Ever After" with the "Boy Next Door," so I thought.

One night, the "Boy Next Door" invited me to his home for dinner. He was a fabulous cook. He introduced me to his family, showed me his castle, and introduced me to his dog, who joined us at the dining table. Unfortunately, I was allergic to the family member with the four paws. The next day as he presented his dowry to me, he asked me if I was going to run for the hills, and I did.

Although we are still in touch, and I consider him a friend and confidant, I was allergic to the dog and could never go to his home without having an asthma attack. I struggled over this issue and knew I didn't want to spend six months falling in love with someone I could not live with. I didn't see how our lives could merge if I had to sleep in another home. I didn't want to get my heart broken. I explained the dog dilemma and as he looked at my JDate profile one last time, he noticed my entry that stated I was not a pet person. He clearly understood. The dog had home court advantage and I couldn't break up their family.

On my last date with "The Boy Next Door," like clockwork, my phone rang and it was the long lost but not forgotten "Latin Lover." Without realizing it, just moments before, he had coincidently left the same restaurant the "Boy Next Door" and I were walking into hand in hand for dinner. How could that happen? It was that magic GPS device again. I told the "Latin Lover" it still remained a very small world and wondered again how his male radar detector automatically turned on when it appeared I was moving on.

Although it didn't work out, I am grateful for meeting the "Boy Next Door." It just gives you hope that no matter what you go through, whether a heartache, a heartbreak, or simply a love affair, there will always be someone who will create a spark in you at any age. You can spend your whole life looking, while there may be a "Boy Next Door" ready to capture your heart if you take the time to notice.

The Flower Boy Song

I had been trading emails for a few weeks with a handsome man who owned a high end Flower Shop on the West Side. He was passionate about flowers and designed many a Hollywood wedding.

The "Flower Boy" and I also shared a passion for music and coincidently both had box seats at the Hollywood Bowl. His box was in the first row. Unfortunately mine was the last box in the house.

I thought about how much money the "Architect" would have saved when we were married if we had met this flower connection earlier. He might have been his biggest account. I wondered how often the "Flower Boy" arrived for a date with flowers in tow, as he didn't have to make a pit stop. After all, wouldn't it be embarrassing to have all those flowers at your finger tips and show up empty handed?

We finally spoke on the phone and instead of having an official date, we had a "pre-date," one where he decided to check me out and screen me in advance before officially asking me out on a date. It was like test driving a car before buying it. The very next night, we both would be dining in our box seats at the Hollywood Bowl for jazz night, and he offered to stop by mine and say hello. I started to wonder if he would walk by mine, decide I didn't make the cut, and keep walking and deliver flowers to another long haired brunette in another box. I hoped that wouldn't be the case. I wondered if he would have any flowers with him, and made sure he knew that my favorite was the Casablanca Lilly.

Five minutes before the performance started, the "Flower Boy" arrived at my box with a bottle of fine red wine. We talked about all the music we had experienced at the Hollywood Bowl over the years. We compared shows we both attended where we never met. He claimed he had attended over 1000 shows at the Bowl. He shared his story as a young boy how he would come to the Hollywood Bowl the first day tickets would go on sale and buy seats on the last bench close to the sky at half price with his allowance he had saved over the years. He obviously had upgraded his lifestyle and sold a lot of flowers. He bragged about his front row box, that someday I might get to see in the event I passed his test.

I told him how I was happy to have seen James Brown, the hardest working man in show business, perform at the Bowl one year, as he sadly passed away a few months later. He replied that he had met James Brown, the day after the singer was released from jail. His introduction however, was in a urinal of the men's room at a local hotel, where the "Flower Boy" asked James, "What's Shakin?"

The "Flower Boy" called me on my cell phone during intermission to say hello and compare show reviews of the previous performance. He ended with "I'll talk to you soon." I didn't expect to hear back from him, but he left a message the next morning with yet another show review of the second half of the evening. But he still did not ask me out for an official date.

It appeared I hadn't passed the test and would never get a floral delivery from the "Flower Boy." I thought perhaps our paths would cross again at an evening at the Hollywood Bowl and that he might stop by to say a friendly hello. Five days after my preview, when he had already become a distant memory, I received a call from the "Flower Boy" and he invited me to be his date for dinner and music at the Bowl later that week. He planned a beautiful picnic and was proud of his VIP parking spot and promised he would spoil me rotten. I realized that sometimes it just takes a while for men to decide if you made the cut or not. The evening at the bowl was delightful and I went home and slept like a baby after enjoying the beautiful music led by conductor John Williams.

Fantasy Island

I recently had a date with a man I met on JDate who advertised meeting him in "JDate's Fantasy Island," a comedic take off on the television series, *Fantasy Island*. It was catchy, he wanted to get noticed, and it turned out he lived a few blocks away. I decided to meet him for lunch.

Our lunch turned out to be a session similar to an AA meeting for cyber-daters. He was a JDate addict and needed guidance and support. His advertisement took him in a direction he didn't expect.

My date told me in great detail about how all of women online communicate in a naughty way in instant messages and on the telephone. It was a bit on the X-rated side of life. He added that he never met these women in person, and only communicated online or on the telephone. Women across the country were contacting him in response to his request for a fantasy life. I wondered if he needed to start a local cyber-dating support group to handle this addiction and if I needed to do an intervention. I assured him that there are many women in cyberspace, myself included, who did not engage in this type of communication and suggested he change his profile to "Great guy looking for loyal and devoted mate and companion." He obviously hadn't read my Profile Definitions.

I felt sorry for him. He was truly a nice guy. What did he expect? He wanted to tell me the details of all of his phone conversations and text message exchanges with the women wanting a fantasy cyber-date. I told him that I hadn't engaged in that type of intimate cyber conversations, nor did any girlfriends of mine that I was aware of. I didn't care if he paid for my valet parking or not, I left the restaurant.

The Plastic Surgeon

I thought I was done with dating men in the medical profession after my failed engagement with the "Neurologist." But when I received an email from a "Plastic Surgeon" who was writing to me during his vacation in New York, a place he originally resided, I thought I would reconsider.

The "Plastic Surgeon" and I shared a passion for travel and especially enjoyed going on cruises. He had posed in his JDate profile in a photograph recently taken on a Crystal Cruise, which one of my favorite ships. He made sure to send me his website so I knew he was truly a board certified "Plastic Surgeon."

I originally agreed to have dinner with him on Sunday night after he returned to Los Angeles, but requested to change it to lunch so I could stay home and watch the closing ceremonies of the Olympics in Beijing. I hoped he would understand.

While waiting for a response from the "Plastic Surgeon" I went back to his website and looked at all the procedures he was offering. I was hoping he wouldn't critique me on the first date and wondered if he would think that I needed any repair work done. He advertised a revolutionary new face lift that claimed to be able to shave eight to ten years off my age in a matter of hours. He could fix my broken veins that would someday appear on my legs. I looked at the "before" and "after" photos and decided I just wasn't ready to sign up yet. I hoped he wouldn't comment on my cute little nose that unfortunately was a bit smaller than the one I had years ago as it had broken and needed to be repaired. His services included limousine service to and from surgery, and all of his procedures could be charged to a credit card where I would receive frequent flyer miles.

I was sure his intentions were sincere, and that our first date would not be like a free consultation that he advertised on his site. Still, I didn't want to drive alone in the dark to downtown L.A. and although he lived over an hour a way, I was hoping we could meet in the daytime.

When the "Plastic Surgeon" called me and agreed to drive to the West Side in the early afternoon so we could both enjoy the closing ceremony of the *Games of the XXIX Olympiad* I was thrilled. Neither of us had seen the Opening Ceremony, but he still had his saved on TiVo and if I was lucky perhaps I could watch it with him one evening if we went past the first date. My mother called in the morning with her loving support and although she is a natural beauty and prides herself in never having any work done, she did say if there was a Plastic Surgeon in the family, she would reconsider.

My first date with the "Plastic Surgeon" was at a restaurant in Century City. We moved straight into the second date without interruption. No we didn't have an overnight two day affair, we simply talked for so long that after a few hours when it was time to order dessert, we mutually agreed it was time to call it the second date so we could talk about things that I preferred not to discuss on a first date. The restaurant didn't have the opportunity to turn over our table to another patron that evening.

The "Plastic Surgeon" was brilliant and I immediately respected him and was in awe of his accomplishments and devotion to his children. Our family values were in synch, and much to our surprise, he also grew up in New Jersey, only two small towns away from me. He didn't live as close as the "Boy Next Door" who stopped calling, but he certainly could be referred to as the "Hometown Boy" should I wish. His father's retail store was down the street from my father's retail store and we immediately bonded. We had the same roots. I had learned from the past how important it is to have those same core values.

Now, there is no such thing as a perfect date. Although his online profile said he was divorced, unfortunately he was separated and recently filed for divorce. He assured me there would be no reconciliation with his soon to be ex-wife. I knew he had a long haul ahead of him and I was concerned about being the "Transition Person" again. He clearly did not have a "T.P." He had only three dates in six months, and I was the third. He was open in telling me about the first one, who didn't look anything like her photos and thought they were from 20 years ago. She ended up "stalking" him and he just wasn't interested. There was the second one who didn't put her weight on her profile, and just had a fairly attractive head shot. When he met her, he was surprised and disappointed that she weighed over 200 pounds. He assumed all cyber-dates were like that. But when he met me, his third date, he told me I looked better than my photos. And of course men are visual and being a man whose profession is making women more beautiful, he was adamant about truth in advertising.

I came clean, as I always do on the first date, and told him my real age and he had no problem with it. I assume he forgot that he advertised he was looking for a woman from 30-40 and I was a decade beyond his limit. Perhaps he didn't know what he wanted yet. At the end of our date he politely asked me if we could go on a "third" date, I happily agreed.

Later that evening he sent me an email to thank me for being true to myself and to him via the Internet. He added that he thought I was a very attractive person both inside and out. He mentioned that he was amazed how our values seemed to align so well. He referred to his experience on his previous two dates where the photos did not add up to the person he met, but that in my case he said the photos were an understatement of my true beauty. He ended his note with, "Thanks for being real."

I went to sleep that night thinking that life was good. The "Plastic Surgeon" wasn't thinking of remodeling me, but perhaps wanted me to be a part of his life and journey. A chapter of hope for both of us was starting. Whether together or apart, we had a successful date and at least we could be friends. He called a few days later and asked me for dinner and we had that "third" date. He was kind enough to drive down to my neighborhood after surgery and it took him an hour and a half to get here. We dined in my favorite local restaurant and watched the sail boats arrive back to their slips from a night of racing. He talked about how much he loved his family and I of course respected him for that. I politely critiqued his profile for him and listened to his story of the difficult divorce process he was going through. Thoughts went back to me sitting in my "war room" while going through my divorce which I did not want to relive. I lent him an ear for support, and politely told him he may not know what he is looking for in a woman just yet. Whatever happens, I know I met a quality man who accepted me for who I was and didn't want to change me. It was refreshing from a man who makes a living out of changing women. Although I did wonder if it was time for another Botox injection as I drove home, I decided it could wait and I could just be me.

CHAPTER 15

The Tango Lesson

It had been well over a month since I heard from the "Latin Lover." He was gone. He was finally living his life off-line, and I was living my life on-line. I often wondered if we hadn't been introduced in person, if he would have viewed my online profile and written to me. I guess I will never know.

While sorting through my in box, I received an invitation for an exciting event, tastings of wine from South America complete with personalized tango lessons. It caught my eye and my mind reflected to a time where learning how to tango was an important part of my life.

Ten years ago, when the former "Love of My Life" and I decided to take a three-week vacation to South America, we decided we could not go to Argentina and not know how to dance the tango. After all, we would be out for the evening, and we wanted to blend in with the locals. Dancing the tango was a must.

I had researched where we could get private lessons on the West Side and found the Ebson School of Dancing, run by Vilma Ebson. The school was actually featured as a cover story on Life magazine in the 1940s. How fortunate for me it was only a few miles away.

Vilma was the younger sister of Buddy Ebson, who starred as Jed Clampett in the television series, *The Beverly Hillbillies*. She was almost 90 years old and she spent most of our lessons reminiscing about all of the old Hollywood Stars she had taught to dance.

Vilma's father owned a dance studio when she was a young child. She was part of a vaudeville dance act with her brother Buddy in the 1920s and appeared in the *Ziegfeld Follies of 1934* as well as other Broadway shows.

Sadly, Vilma just passed away in March of 2007 at the age of 96. I saw her obituary in the newspaper and was saddened by reading it. I thought she would live to be 100 and that perhaps I could go back for a refresher with the "Latin Lover" someday.

As Vilma slowly moved, with a smile on her face, she was determined that we'd be experts in tango before we left for Buenos Aires.

We arrived in Argentina a little overconfident after being professionally taught. As we were about to take the floor at Bar Sur, a tango club for the locals in the San

Telmo section of Buenos Aires, I got cold feet. We were American tourists among the most serious tango dancers. I decided to take a pass and perhaps go back to Vilma when I returned to California so I could graduate to an advanced level of tango dancing.

When I first met the "Latin Lover" he asked me if I would like to take tango lessons with him. An expert dancer himself, and a former instructor, tango was something he still wanted to master and he wanted me to be his partner on the dance floor.

I told him the story of Vilma Ebson and how only a year earlier she had passed away and that I didn't know any other instructors. He added it to the list of things we never got to do.

So when the invitation arrived for the Wine and Tango soiree, I was hopeful the "Latin Lover" would still be interested in tango dancing with me. I sent him an email with the invitation asking him if he would join me, and he replied an hour later with one word and said, "Sure!"

I went upstairs to my wardrobe closet and picked out the perfect tango dress and started to fantasize about the film, *Last Tango in Paris* as I practiced the steps nightly in preparation before I went to sleep.

Suddenly a second invitation arrived in the mail for a "Tapas and Tango" evening at a social club I belong to. I was surrounded by tango everywhere, and wished I hadn't ended the relationship with the "Latin Lover" as there was no one else I could imagine perfecting the art of tango with.

With our date three weeks away, I didn't expect the "Latin Lover" would come through. He had a history of cancelling and he had stopped calling for some time now. This was not an event one could attend as a solo act. I was hopeful he would reappear for our last and final tango, but either way, in memory of Vilma, I would tango once again.

The day before the tango lesson was one of many celebrations in Los Angeles. I had the opportunity to bid farewell to a 250 million dollar satellite rocket that had just finished being built. It was about to be sent on a journey to the equator near Singapore where it will be launched 22,000 miles into the sky to find its new home for the next 15 years. The satellite, *Galaxy 19* would be transmitting television, video, audio, and of course emails of many potential cyber-dates. It was possible I could meet my true love through this amazing piece of technology. A select few were invited and I was thrilled to be a part of the celebration and rocket signing ceremony. I sipped champagne to toast the event and left for the second major celebration of the day, the grand opening of the new Neiman Marcus store in the Valley.

Women all over Los Angeles had been excited about this day for two years. We waited for the invitation to arrive in the mail so it could be added to our social calendars. It was a celebration so grand that limos filled with beautiful women from all over Southern California arrived on opening night. Proceeds from the party would support several charitable organizations including ALS, the Museum of Contemporary Art, The Children's Burn Center, and the New West Symphony. It was the night before the tango lesson, and on my way to the gala store opening, I finally called the "Latin Lover" to see if he would be accompanying me or not. If he would not be attending, I needed to find a Plan B for the evening. I was discussing this dilemma with my girlfriend in the cosmetics department, and she came up with a brilliant suggestion. His name was Emilio. Emilio was my Plan B. Emilio was born and raised in Argentina. Emilio learned to tango as an infant, he was handsome and single, and she was sure he would love to be my tango partner the following evening. Suddenly, I felt better that the evening would not be a disaster and I agreed to have her call Emilio.

With Plan B almost in place, I didn't even mind if the "Latin Lover" stood me up. Although I would have been disappointed, I realized my life did not revolve around a date with my former beau who may have been considering other options for the evening. On my way home, my cell phone rang, and yes, it was indeed the "Latin Lover." He had resurfaced less than 24 hours before the big event to confirm we would be going together. My face suddenly was replaced with a joyful smile and I was excited thinking about our upcoming tango lesson.

Our reunion after over a month apart could have been awkward, but it was not. We sipped wines from Argentina, Brazil, and Chile, and he suggested taking me on a trip in December to Argentina. He told me how much he had missed me. We had our private tango lesson and a photographer snapped photos of us on the dance floor. The "Latin Lover" was so happy to see me that he signed us up to take another tango lesson the following week. He booked several more dates with me for romantic weekend getaways that very night. We came back to my house where our cars reconnected like best friends in the garage. We collaborated musically as I played Beatles and Frank Sinatra songs on the piano and he sang the lyrics. It was as if no time had passed at all.

I fell asleep comfortably in his arms in a candle lit room and realized it is true what they say, "It Takes Two to Tango."

CHAPTER 16

The Engagement Ring

The Four C's (or Are There Five?)

Nothing is more exciting than when you announce you are engaged to your friends and family. I have done this a few times as you know.

Once notified, the women immediately grab your hand and examine the rock you are now wearing. It's a wonder women don't have their own copy of the *Rappaport Sheet*, the diamond industry's world-wide price list, or even a jeweler's loop in their purses or briefcases, the examination is so intense.

It's no different than if a woman announces she is pregnant and strangers attempt to rub her belly. The same theory goes to the shiny rock on the left hand finger representing you are now a fiancée.

It's a ritual most women go through at some point in their lives. Although I have been proposed to officially four times, and unofficially a few more, I was the recipient of four rings ranging in size from approximately one carat to four carats. As I got older, the sizes got bigger. I never liked large jewelry when I was a child. My mother always told me not to worry, that I would grow into it, and she was right.

Noticing this phenomenon and ratio between age and carat size, I suddenly subscribed to the "carat per decade" rule, something I thought was funny at first. I noticed younger brides getting an upgrade on that important 10 and 25 year anniversary mark. As I received a beautiful four carat diamond at 49, just shy of my 50th birthday, I believed my carat per decade theory actually to be true.

Every woman knows the 4 C's of a diamond: color, cut, clarity, and carat. Every man fears the conversation about the 4 C's and tries not to have topic become a part of their daily vocabulary or go into a jewelry store prematurely. The former "Love of My Life" was allergic to jewelry stores and he made it a point just not to enter one, fearing the commitment was there if he went in for a viewing. He was so frightened of jewelry stores; it wasn't until our seventh and last year together that he finally bought me a piece of jewelry.

However, I believe there should be 5 C's with the 5th being "commitment." Yes, the commitment of "til death do us part and to be together forever, for better or worse." Of course there should be a 5th C, when shopping for a ring, so why doesn't anyone ever talk about that? Why are there only 4 C's? Why are there so many failed marriages, and former fiancées floating around?

While I was engaged, I was proud to be a fiancée, planning a wedding, soon to be a bride and a wife. It never occurred to me that I would be a statistic and the 5th "C" would go out the window.

When an engagement is over and the couple does not end up walking down the aisle, one usually questions what happened to the engagement ring. Quite often the first question a woman is asked when newly "unengaged" is if she kept the ring. Similarly, the first question a man is asked under the same circumstance is if he got the ring back. Why do people care about the status of a ring? Two people are aching in pain over their loss and others only care about the whereabouts of a ring. How insensitive I thought, but many of us are all guilty of asking that question. It is no different than asking a new mother if she had a boy or a girl.

Recently I ran into an old friend who was no longer engaged. Her fiancé had ended their engagement on a voicemail. She looked well and had recovered from the breakup and her ex-fiancé had long since gotten married to another. We started talking and the subject of her engagement ring came up. I asked her what happened to her three carat Tiffany round and she advised me that she had kept the ring. Years later, she added, it was sold on eBay to a young couple about to get engaged who met on Match.com.

After listening to her story, I decided to do a little further investigating on the subject and was surprised to find out that in the world of happily never after, there are engagement laws that vary depending on what state you live in.

Although I am not an attorney, it is my understanding that if you live in the state of Montana, an engagement ring is considered a gift. Even if the couple doesn't walk down the aisle, the woman gets to keep the ring. If I were a man, I'd consider buying a smaller ring, and give my wife a fabulous upgrade on our first anniversary.

In other states such as Iowa, Kansas, Michigan, New Jersey, New Mexico, New York, Pennsylvania, and Wisconsin, I am told the ring goes back to the donor, typically the man, if the engagement is off regardless of who dumped who, unless plans are agreed upon otherwise.

However, in the state of California, where we always claim to be different from the rest of the country, I learned that if the man breaks the engagement, he doesn't get the ring back. Sorry guys, you really need to be sure before you put a ring on a woman's finger as you will have to be prepared to lose it if you back out.

If the ring is a family heirloom, it should go back into the family from where it once came from regardless of who dumped who.

And so the story goes of the 4 or 5 C's and the saga of many engagement rings that quite often end up being sold on eBay or on a new website called idonowidont.com, to young lovers with high hopes who have met in cyberspace.

CHAPTER 17

And Then Came BlackBerry

Coming from an age where a blackberry was part of my fruit salad, it's now an everyday way of life. I feel it is so sad, that people go out in public and never notice those who walk by because they are immersed in texting or returning emails on their BlackBerry's.

I am also guilty of this phenomenon as I have had my BlackBerry for over one year now so I can get email when I am not at home or out of town. With the traffic in Los Angeles, I didn't realize how handy this little device would be. We are living in a town of BlackBerry addicts. My BlackBerry now notifies me if I have an email from a potential male suitor, or a "flirt" from an interested party on JDate or a "wink" from another on Match. I find out immediately if someone adds me to their "hot list." In the world of information overload, it is too much data coming too soon. Often I don't know whether to delete it or if I should go home immediately in anticipation to find out who is waiting for me in my in box; after all, it could be "the one."

Just yesterday, I was sitting in the lounge of the Peninsula Hotel waiting for a friend, reading my email, and I looked up and there was a handsome man sitting at the table next to me. A man I will never meet, because he was fixated on his BlackBerry as well and he didn't notice me. We never made eye contact. I looked around the room and half of the people were engaged in interesting conversations so it appeared, yet those alone, just can't be alone. We are all connecting and disconnecting on the BlackBerry.

The cute guy left without noticing me and was replaced by another handsome patron, a former NBA basketball player who had two mobile devices on the table in front of him. He starts to text someone when I interrupted his train of thought and asked him, "Why don't you just pick up the phone and talk to them?" He looked at me curiously, and said, "Do you think so? " I replied, "Yes, it is bad "netiquette" to text someone and expect them to immediately reply."

So our conversation started. First we talked about how the Los Angeles Lakers had a disappointing loss against the Boston Celtics in the NBA finals. Then we talked about how sad it was that Red Auerbach, former General Manager of the Celtics, didn't get to see his team win another championship. He had sadly passed away a year and a half earlier and had 16 NBA Championships during his tenure.

Finally our conversation went to the subject of love, life, family, and why people can't seem to stay in relationships for too long as they think there is something better around the corner. This is the new "one-up" concept I so dislike. If we are living in a land of one up's and trade up's how do we ever meet "the one" and stay together? People go on cyber-dates that seem to go well, knowing that perhaps the one you may meet on the following day will be better. It's no wonder it is so hard for people to make a commitment.

I don't like this behavior at all. This conversation was causing me concern. Being a serial monogamist, and not a serial dater, I had no idea this was the reality in the dating market. I told him the story of the "Flirty Guy" who would only text me, and he disagreed with me in holding firm to receive a phone call. He thought I should text him back and "hook up." We obviously had different values, I thought.

Perhaps it is just that men and women are wired so differently. As a woman I want to be with only one man. According to this man, it is just unnatural for a man to be with only one woman. It is a struggle, a losing battle so he said, while juggling our conversation and his two mobile devices at the same time.

I thought about how loyal the "Neurologist" was to me, and even my "Architect" husband never strayed with another woman. Did I just get lucky and have men who felt I was woman enough in the past? How do I find that kind of value system moving forward while everyone is receiving a text of the next possible cyber-date? I was feeling confused. The basketball player was married for almost 25 years. I didn't ask if he was loyal or not. I didn't want to know.

It's been over one year since the "Neurologist" broke our engagement. One day recently in my in box he reappeared as a member of my online dating site. The computer decided we'd be a good match. Apparently we were both back online looking for a love to replace the one we once had and had not yet been successful. They say timing is everything. I have experienced meeting the right person at the wrong time and meeting the wrong person at the right time. It is now time to get the balance right and finally meet the right man at the right time. Hopefully with my rules of "netiquette" in tow, I will succeed. And as I hum the words of my daily mantra of "I Will Survive" courtesy of Gloria Gaynor, I am grateful that I have survived the Perils of Cyber-Dating and I remain a hopeful romantic whether online, on the ground, and wherever I may roam.

Acknowledgements

I wrote this book to highly encourage any single person with an email address to find "the one" on an Internet dating site. I wouldn't be writing a juicy-tell-all if I didn't believe I could make a difference in the lives of others.

With over 40 million singles online now in search of love, I felt the need to share my stories so those would not feel alone in cyberspace. I write about love, dating, and relationships in a Web 2.0 world where all the traditions and rules have changed. I have received such an overwhelming support for this book, and I'm forever grateful to all those who have encouraged me on my journey.

I want to thank my wonderful family for their support. I may have not picked the best husbands, but I certainly was blessed with the best parents in the world who have provided me their unconditional love throughout my life.

An extra special thank you goes to my supportive girlfriend network who listened to my stories over the years and continued to laugh while I was on the verge of tears. The list is too big to name, but you know who you are and I thank you from the bottom of my heart. I'd also like to thank my coaches and mentors, Roger Chiocchi, Frances Greenberg, Henry Kavett, and Heather Jumah for their constant encouragement and support. I am thankful to Brad Nye, who brought me into the Venice Interactive Community in the early days, and helped me choose the title of this book back in 1995. I am especially grateful to the women in my Ladies Who Launch Incubator who inspired me to finish writing this book as well as creating CyberDatingExpert.com a social networking site for those to share their online dating experiences. In addition, I want to thank the supportive members of An Empowered Woman, Step Up Women's Network, the Costume Council at LACMA, The Beverly Hills Women's Club, The Council for the Library Foundation of Los Angeles, Women in Film, the Young Literati of the Library Foundation, and my friends on Facebook as well as my business associates on LinkedIn. A special thank you goes to Veronica De Laurentiis and our Monday night women's group, Diane Sutter who orchestrates our Cool Chicks group, as well as Dr. Pat Allen, Dr. Judi Bloom, E. Jean Carroll, Robyn Carter, Diane Dimond, Julie Ferman, Patrick McMullan, Denise Oliver, Greg Rubinstein, Barbara Segal, Donna Sozio, and Cheryl Woodcock. And to my publishers at Morgan James – Rick Frishman and David Hancock along with Margo Toulouse, thank you for insuring that this book would be released in time for Valentines Day.

And although bitter sweet as it is, I have to thank the men I met on my journey – for without them, this book could not be possible and the lessons would not have been learned. And last, I'd like to thank Oprah Winfrey who now gives everyone permission to turn "30" on their "50th" birthdays. Enjoy!

About the Author

Julie Spira started her career as a radio show host and voice-over announcer. She holds a Bachelor of Science degree in Television-Radio from the Roy H. Park School of Communications at Ithaca College, Ithaca, N.Y. Spira was an executive for several radio syndication companies as well as the RKO Radio Networks.

As a serial entrepreneur, Spira was a pioneer in the Internet industry both personally and professionally. She was involved with several Internet startups starting in the mid 1990s. As an early adopter of the Internet, Spira has almost 15 years of online dating experience on multiple dating websites. Spira was on the Internet before most people knew there was an Internet – or at least it felt that way to her in 1994. By default, she became an expert at cyber-dating. Her cyber-dating experiences encompassed the time period from her 30s to her 50s. The author proves you can be desirable as a single woman looking for love online at any age. With the combination of her technology background and her personal experiences, she hopes that women and men of all ages can learn from and relate to her stories of cyber-dating. Spira hosts the radio show, "Ask the Cyber-Dating Expert." She sits on the board of several non-profit organizations in Los Angeles and is a gifted mentor and philanthropist.

We would love to hear about your Online Dating experiences

Come and share your online dating stories at CyberDatingExpert.com

Cyber Wedding Album – If you found "The One" and got married to someone you met on an Internet dating site, you may be considered for inclusion in our Cyber Wedding Album. We will feature your wedding photos in a video montage to share the exciting news. Please send your information and photos with the site you met on to weddings@cyberdatingexpert.com.

Cyber Love Stories – Every day we meet couples who have met online and have a happy story to share. For inclusion as a Cyber Love Story, please let us know at love@cyberdatingexpert.com.

Peril of the Week – Oops! Did someone break one of the Rules of Netiquette or did you experience a cyber-dating mishap? Let us know, and if it's time to say, "Next!" please submit your story to perils@cyberdatingexpert.com.

Cyber-Dating Coaching – If you need help with your online profile, send us an email to coaching@cyberdatingexpert.com.

BUY A SHARE OF THE FUTURE IN YOUR COMMUNITY

These certificates make great holiday, graduation and birthday gifts that can be personalized with the recipient's name. The cost of one S.H.A.R.E. or one square foot is $54.17. The personalized certificate is suitable for framing and will state the number of shares purchased and the amount of each share, as well as the recipient's name. The home that you participate in "building" will last for many years and will continue to grow in value.

Here is a sample SHARE certificate:

YES, I WOULD LIKE TO HELP!

I support the work that Habitat for Humanity does and I want to be part of the excitement! As a donor, I will receive periodic updates on your construction activities but, more importantly, I know my gift will help a family in our community realize the dream of homeownership. **I would like to SHARE in your efforts against substandard housing in my community!** *(Please print below)*

PLEASE SEND ME _____ SHARES at $54.17 EACH = $ $_____

In Honor Of: _____

Occasion: (Circle One)   HOLIDAY   BIRTHDAY   ANNIVERSARY

       OTHER: _____

Address of Recipient: _____

Gift From: _____ *Donor Address:* _____

Donor Email: _____

I AM ENCLOSING A CHECK FOR $ $_____ PAYABLE TO HABITAT FOR HUMANITY <u>OR</u> PLEASE CHARGE MY VISA OR MASTERCARD *(CIRCLE ONE)*

Card Number _____ Expiration Date: _____

Name as it appears on Credit Card _____ Charge Amount $ _____

Signature _____

Billing Address _____

Telephone # Day _____ Eve _____

PLEASE NOTE: Your contribution is tax-deductible to the fullest extent allowed by law.
Habitat for Humanity • P.O. Box 1443 • Newport News, VA 23601 • 757-596-5553
www.HelpHabitatforHumanity.org

Printed in the USA
CPSIA information can be obtained
at www.ICGtesting.com
JSHW022123060524
62644JS00001B/176